MW01295257

will blessed by the book. May you [?] grew in the knowledge of God's love & may His word continue to dwell in you richly.

GOD'S FINANCES—
A MATTER OF
THE HEART

J. Boudoin

xulon PRESS

TABLE OF CONTENTS

INTRODUCTION

For years, I have heard ministers speak about tithes and offerings only during the time that was set aside in the service to receive the tithe and offerings. When the time for offering came, it was an associate Minister or someone else that gave the scripture or prayer, not the Pastor. It was as if the Pastor did not want to be associated with this time of the service. The short message or appeal to let everyone know that it was time to give went something like this: "Now let's continue in the spirit of worship by giving our tithes and offering to God". The focus was on the requirement to tithe because we needed to "give God what is due to Him". The typical scripture references I recall were Malachi 3: 8-12 and Luke 6:38. The full context of these scriptures was rarely explored, however from the pulpit. Instead, certain aspects of the scriptures were emphasized. I recall the short exerts or emphasis placed on "robbing God" and Him "opening up the windows of heaven" to bless me. The emotions that I usually felt were guilt and hope. I felt guilty about not giving because I was robbing God and at the same time I had hope of a fruitful return if I did give. The problem is that these feelings that I had were not anything based on truth, revelation or knowledge of the Word. They were simply fleshly emotions and thoughts merely responding to what I heard. So, the offering time was an emotional event rather than a spiritual one for me. The true spirit of tithe and offering was not there for me. I'm sure that I am not alone in these feelings. The result of this is that we have many Christians that are ignorant concerning God's plans for their finances. For years I thought that these were the only scriptures on finances in the Bible. I don't recall many sermons on giving, tithing, finances or how to manage the 90% that I was left with after tithing. I do recall many "sermonettes" (5 minutes exhortation) about the subject, but not any sound teaching on the topic. My assumption was that God was only concerned about the 10% that "was due to Him".

The biblical perspective of money tends to make people feel guilty in today's marketplace. I believe this happens because people believe that it is their money and it is no one's business how they manage it. As long as they give the tithe, then they feel that the church shouldn't be concerned. Therefore, this topic is often ignored, unexplained or even more dangerous, it is misinterpreted. Most people don't look to the Bible for financial instruction. Again, I believe that this is because of our view that the money belongs to us. Additionally, the fact that we don't hear messages on money and are not afforded the opportunity gain additional insights via workshops offered through the local church leads the people to believe it is not a critical element in our spiritual walk. There are twice as many verses on money than on faith and prayer combined!! Obviously, God thinks that it is important and it must have *some* relationship to our spiritual walk. I long for the day when we here teaching and preaching about finances with the same fervor we do about faith, prayer, joy, salvation, etc!

In the past couple of years, 3 John 2 has become the theme scripture for biblical prosperity—*Beloved, I wish above all things that thou mayest prosper and be in health, even as thy soul prospereth.* It has been taught in such a way now that it has influenced many believers to think that it is the one key to financial success. In addition, a lot of Christians also believe that this is the fundamental scripture reference for prosperity today. The scripture has been taken out of context. Many believers have been led to believe that it is the will of God that we all prosper in terms of money. Many people have placed their emotions and hope on gaining prosperity and fully place the expectations on God to make it happen. The accountability on the part of the individual is somehow overlooked. So now the motive for giving is no longer that we owe God, but primarily because we feel that He will reward us with prosperity if we do.

What has happened to change the mentality of the church towards personal finances? I believe that a critical missing element in the body of Christ today is thorough teaching on finances from God's perspective. The people of God are hanging on to the popular scriptures on giving yet they remain ignorant concerning the requirements of discipline, self control, prayer and stewardship. The objective of this book is to provide basic principles to challenge your thoughts, ideas and traditions regarding finances. The truth is that God has a lot to say about finances in His Word. Why then is it not being taught to the body of Christ? Why are we hung up only on prosperity? Why aren't specific prayers for financial wisdom uttered during altar call? Why do we ask God for financial blessings when the plan for achieving it is not being followed? Why are people of faith not living in prosperity? Why are we in financial bondage? There are fundamental truths that are being neglected in the teaching of financial freedom and prosperity. There are very subtle, yet powerful habits, thoughts, behaviors and attitudes that are going unchecked. The result is financial bondage and the inability to worship God freely. I believe that it is a specific trick of the enemy to keep the people of God ignorant concerning the true motives and beliefs regarding finances and the subsequent actions in their daily life that follow these beliefs.

This book will challenge you to explore those hidden truths regarding your finances and bring you face to face with root causes of your current financial condition. It will lead you down a path to identify them and conquer them according to the Word of God. The path is simply to reveal to you the truth about the lies you are being told to you by the enemy about your financial condition and beliefs. There are budgeting tips included, but **you cannot properly construct an effective budget unless you unlock the strongholds that are in your mind about money, finances, stewardship, giving, spending and prosperity.** It you do not deal with these issues, you will build them into your budget, which will significantly delay or defeat your efforts to achieving your financial goals. I pray that you allow the Word of God to minister to you freely and openly as you read this book. At the end of the book you will find worksheets that are designed to assist you in your journey. It is very important that you take the time to complete each worksheet. Now, let's hear what the Spirit is saying to you, the church.

CHAPTER 1
GOD'S VIEW OF YOUR FINANCES

In order to change your financial condition, you must first obtain the mindset of God related to your finances. There are some basic truths that must be laid as the foundation before you can build your financial house and establish wealth. **Without understanding wealth and money from God's perspective, the path to the abundant life will seem hard and unattainable**. Before you proceed any further, I encourage you to take a moment to pray that your spiritual eyes and ears be opened to receive the things you are about to read. Please do so now. The reason I paused for prayer at this time is because there is a fierce enemy that has placed enormous strongholds, lies, barriers and myths in our minds regarding money. It will take the Spirit of God to move in your hearts and minds to destroy them and replace them with the truth. The fact that you have chosen to read this book means that you are serious about pursuing God's financial plan for your life. While reading this book, you can be assured that the enemy of your soul will remind you of past financial failures, current barriers, current credit reports, past sins and familiar thoughts to hinder your progress in this area. Please pause to pray again. This time, I ask that you pray specifically that those things not be a hindrance to you while you take this journey. After you pray, serve the enemy notice that you bind up those thoughts now. Take time now to complete the worksheet titled My Financial Thoughts. This worksheet will serve as an acknowledgement by you of how you really view money. This is an important step in that you must confess your beliefs. You cannot change what you do not acknowledge.

The Proper Perspective

- *Psalm 24:1 The earth is the LORD's, and the fullness thereof.*
- *Psalm 135:6 Whatsoever the LORD pleased, that did He in heaven, and in earth, in the seas, and all deep places.*
- *Psalm 8:6 Thou madest him to have dominion over the works of thy hands; thou hast put all things under his feet.*

The first thing that we must understand is that God is the sole owner of EVERYTHING. Now, take a moment to think about that. God does not share ownership with anyone. Everything belongs to Him. There is a tendency on the part of mankind to think that only what exists in heaven belongs to God. David offers a simple, yet glorious, reminder in Psalm 24 that the earth too belongs to God. The sovereignty of God is implied here as well. This means that the earth itself and everything that calls earth its home belongs to God. If the earth is His, then He can choose to do with it and its inhabitants and resources as He chooses (Psalm 135:6). We must fully have this perspective in mind when we consider our finances. The money and the things that it buys all belong to God!!! It is **not** our money!!! It belongs to God!!! Now, you may be thinking that that is "super spiritual" talk. Well, it is simply the truth. We have to embrace and accept this fact as the foundation before we can move forward.

Now we know that God is a Spirit and therefore, He is not here physically exchanging His money for goods and services or negotiating contracts. Although He is the sole owner of everything, He has given us the authority to be stewards over His possessions (Psalm 8:6). When someone gives you the authority to take possession of something that belongs rightfully to them, you then have the freedom to handle it on their behalf. For example, let's assume that your friend owns a parcel of land and they give you dominion over it. Your friend has in essence given you the power, authority and control of the land. He also provides you with a very simple contract that gives you some guidelines on how to appropriately use the land.

The contract simply serves as a reminder that you don't actually own the land, but you have a great deal of freedom on running the land within the contractual guidelines set forth. Now because you don't actually own the land, but you have been told you have this dominion, you begin to take steps to make use of the land. You begin to have conversations with potential buyers and business owners. You are making deals that would be in the best interest of your friend because he has entrusted the care of the land to you with a lot of latitude to make decisions while providing some limitations. You are also mindful that your friend has great expectations of care and consideration being given to the land. In the back of your mind throughout all of the negotiations, you know that it is not your land. This is how it is with God. As we are making financial decisions, it should always be in the forefront of our mind that it is not our money, it belongs to God. He has provided some simple instructions in the contract—His Word- for us to follow. He has placed the responsibility and accountability with us to care for His possessions.

The Nature of Money

Money itself has no inherent value. It is neither good nor evil, it is neutral. Money is also not wealth. It can, however, serve as a symbol of wealth. If a person has one million dollars in several locations in their house or in a bank, it does not mean that the person is wealthy. It can remain in the bank or under a mattress for years and never be spent on anything. Is the person still wealthy? Having the tangible money does not make the person wealthy. The same one million dollars can be burned and therefore not spent on anything. If the money is spent to buy houses, cars, jewelry, etc., then it has ascribed value or value has been attributed to the money. We typically say that someone is wealthy based on the things that they have. If someone has an old vehicle, live in a modest home and wear inexpensive jewelry, we would not categorize him or her as wealthy. That person could very well consider himself or herself wealthy based on their own standards. Wealth can be very subjective. Some may not consider the same person wealthy by looking at them outwardly. But the same individual could have several million in assets. Most people consider someone wealthy when the money is exchanged for goods or services. The money can be donated to charity or used to fund a medical school. The same money can be used to purchase drugs or fund gang activity. The value of the money does not change. The money itself is not good or bad. In both cases the moral standards of the person who has the money is the issue, not the money itself.

The problem with money is the devotion that people have to it. When you are devoted to something, your time, talents, energy, efforts and desires are dedicated to it. With these intense feelings toward money and what it can acquire, we begin to develop a love towards it. This affection again is not toward the money itself, but what it can buy—power, prestige, status, satisfaction. It then, in effect, begins to compete with other things in your life that require or request your attention, time, talent, energy, effort and desire. This competition may be with your family, your personal growth, your church/ministry, your personal relationship and fellowship with God or your peace.

Paul in giving encouragement, warning and instruction to Timothy regarding his ministry specifically mentions the pitfalls of this devotion to money. He states *And having food and raiment, let us be therewith content. But they that will be rich fall into temptation and a snare, and into many foolish and hurtful lusts, which drown men in destruction and perdition. For the love of money is the root of all evil: which while some coveted after, they have erred from the faith, and pierced themselves through with many sorrows* (I Timothy 6:8-10). Let's study the message here. First of all, Paul speaks of being content with the necessities of life—food and clothing. He doesn't say that these necessities have to be the bare necessities or not very expensive. He's saying be content that the needs of food, clothing and shelter have been provided no matter how good they are. Again, he is not saying that we should have the bare necessities, he's just saying that whatever the quality and cost of the provision for food and clothing are we should be content with it. He goes on to warn that those that desire to get rich run a serious risk of falling into temptation and a trap. Those that do not find a place of contentment with what they have but desire to be rich will surely be tempted. Paul says that they will be tempted and give in to the temptation. He says that this is akin to falling into a trap which further leads to giving in to many unwise and painful desires that cause them to be destroyed. How can all of these bad things be a result of simply wanting to be rich? Well, the answer is in verse 10. These things occur because of the love of money or the devotion to money. **The desire to be rich is because one's time, talents, efforts, energy and emotions are all geared towards obtaining things that symbolize wealth. These things are obtained with money. If your love and devotion is to obtaining money in order to get rich, then your loyalties are divided.** You cannot be devoted to God and money at the same time. Jesus said in Luke 16:13 that *No servant can serve two masters: for either he will hate the one, and love the other; or else he will hold to the one, and despise the other. Ye cannot serve God and mammon.*

If money is your master in that you do whatever it takes to get it, then you love it more than you love God. The intensity and love we should have for God is described in Deuteronomy 6:4 *Hear, O Israel: The LORD our God is one LORD: And thou shalt love the LORD thy God with all thine heart, and with all thy soul, and with all thy might.* If our mind is constantly planning how to obtain money and our physical bodies are consumed with the acts of getting it, then we cannot possibly devote ourselves completely to the things of God. If we say that we love God then we must obey the requirement to love Him based on His definition of love. If we consume our life's activities with getting money, then we love the money more. Remember, it is really not the money that we are after, rather it is the status, things, position, influence, etc. that money represents to us. Let's look at a practical example. Joan has a good job that meets her needs and she lives comfortably in an apartment. She is not lacking in any material needs at this point in her life. She attends Bible study regularly and is active in the youth ministry as a mentor to young girls. Joan decides that she wants a more luxurious vehicle, new jewelry and a new bedroom set. There is also a host of electronic gadgets that she would like to have to fill up her entertainment center. In order to get these things, Joan must work quite a bit of overtime and maybe get a part time job. The additional hours that she will have to work adds up to 4 hours per day and now she will begin working on Saturdays. These hours will require her to miss Bible study. She will also have to resign as a mentor since she won't be able to meet with the girls weekly, as required. Because Joan is devoted and dedicated to obtaining these items, she decides to devote her time, energy and efforts to working the hours required to get them. She has in effect decided that she loves these things and will do whatever it takes to devote her time and energy to getting them. She cannot physically continue with Bible study, the mentoring program and work overtime, so she had to make a choice. She chose the one she loves the most. She would never say "I love these things more than I love the things of God" because that *sounds* very bad. But, by her actions, she has in fact said it. The things have become her master and she is serving them.

Think about what your efforts are devoted to and determine if you are becoming a slave to money or the things it can buy. Jesus instructed the rich young ruler *"If thou wilt be perfect, go and sell that thou hast, and give to the poor, and thou shalt have treasure in heaven: and come and follow me"* (Matthew 19:21). Jesus was not interested in the ruler selling his possessions because it was a requirement to be poor to follow Jesus. Don't believe that lie! **Jesus wanted the ruler to remove money and his possessions from the throne of his heart so that He could reside there.** Again, the problem was not the money, but the place money held in his heart. How does this love of money lead to temptation and the trap? This happens because our heart becomes filled with the desires of the things that money can buy. We know that *The heart is deceitful above all things, and desperately wicked: who can know it? (Jeremiah 17:9).* The love for money can become deeply rooted in our heart. Once it takes root, the desire will consume our heart and the actions to fulfill the desires will ultimately follow. You begin to act out or live out what is truly in your heart. **The heart or emotions are leading your actions and we often do not subject our actions to spiritual discernment. Your own voice and the determinations of your heart drown out the voice of God speaking through the Holy Spirit in you.** This all leads to making unwise decisions that are outside of the will of God. For Christians, these decisions seem okay because we are not hurting anyone, cursing God or committing any of those other "higher classes of sin" that we think exist. This is the trap!!! The enemy assists us in justifying the actions by telling us that we deserve these things. He may say that as a child of God, we are entitled to have these nice things. While that may be true, we should consult God as to the timing of having those things and if it is truly His will for us at all. Omitting this crucial step can lead to moving forward in the trap. The actions appear to be harmless on the surface. It's just a few extra hours right? It's a trap because you don't see what it really behind it and what it can really lead to. The subtle trap that this can lead to may look something like this:

- obtaining more credit
- creating more debt
- spending more time away from home and family
- increased fatigue
- lower immune system due to lack of sufficient sleep
- physical illness can occur
- less time for devotion with God
- less time in worship
- less time for involvement in ministry
- less quality family time
- less time in fellowship with the saints
- potentially more anxiety
- additional distractions emotionally

The list can go on and on. The root of all of this is the love or devotion to money. Too often, we don't count up the true cost of obtaining things. Take some time to reflect on this list again.

The enemy keeps us blind to the traps that the love of money can lead to. These traps are directly related to money, but you must have a heightened sense of awareness of the motives behind your spending to uncover the hidden danger. Many times, the very thing that we were trying to obtain becomes a curse because it has become an idol. Jesus said in Mark 10:23-25 that having riches can *potentially* keep you from entering the kingdom of God. He said that "*it is easier for a camel to go through the eye of a needle than for a rich man to enter into the kingdom of God*". In other words, there can be a spiritual cost to having riches. Keep in mind that this scripture follows the interaction that He had with the young ruler. The issue with the young ruler was not the things that he had, but rather his devotion to the things that he had. Immediately after the young ruler walked away, Jesus turned to His disciples to share this principle. He was pointing to the young ruler's refusal to give up love of the possessions as an example of the serious hold and power that the things had on him. Jesus was saying in essence, "see how this young man's heart is tied to the possessions and not to Me. The possessions have replaced the desire for Me and that will prohibit him for joining Me in My kingdom." The temptation to hold on to things will be similar in anyone who has an abundance of wealth. This is what will make it hard for him to enter into the kingdom of God. I want to pause here and note parenthetically, that this scripture does **not** say that rich people cannot enter into the kingdom of God. He is saying that is an extremely hard thing for a rich man to enter into a place where God reigns and rules over his life. He powerfully states in the very next sentence (v. 27) *And Jesus looking upon them saith, With men it is impossible, but not with God: for with God all things are possible.* Jesus is saying that truly it is a hard thing for man to do on his own, but with God's grace, it is possible. What a high price to pay for the devotion to money! Thanks be to God for 2nd Peter 1:3.

> *According as his divine power hath given unto us all things that pertain unto life and godliness, through the knowledge of him that hath called us to glory and virtue: ⁴Whereby are given unto us exceeding great and precious promises: that by these ye might be partakers of the divine nature, having escaped the corruption that is in the world through lust.*

The promises of God provide a way of escape from the temptations that draw us away. We have to realize that God has given us all things that we need in this life already. I encourage you to meditate on this scripture.

It is fitting that I also review the extreme view by some Christians that it is never God's desire for us to have a lot of money or to be rich. This is not true. Mark 10:23-25 and 1st Timothy 6:8-10 are often the scriptures used to support this position. As you read above, this is not the intent of the teaching. We have somehow missed the point of the teaching. This is another subtle trick of the enemy to keep Christians in poverty. . As you can now see, it is not the money itself that the Word of God warns us against, it is the place the money can hold in our heart. It is truly a matter of the heart. God desires to be first in our lives, not second. When He is not first, then we have placed our hope, expectation and desires in what is first.

CHAPTER 2

STEWARDSHIP—WHO'S MONEY IS IT ANYWAY?

There aren't many messages preached today on the topic of stewardship concerning personal finances. Many references to stewardship today are limited to accountability of church property and ministry. If it is related to personal finances, it is only mentioned in terms of the tithe. Since God owns everything as stated earlier, and He has placed us as stewards over His possessions, then that includes everything that He owns. In the Old Testament a steward was over the master's entire household affairs. He was responsible for the management, upkeep and production of every aspect of the household, including the finances. God has appointed all Christians to be His stewards on earth. Stewardship is not an option—dominion was *given* to us. When we were given dominion, the accountability that goes with it was placed on us as well. The responsibility of stewardship is inherent in the fact that the earth does not belong to us. Let's review this—

- God owns everything
- God is a Spirit—He's not handling transactions physically on earth
- God has entrusted His followers with the responsibility to manage His possessions on earth.

Along with this responsibility comes accountability. As the parable of the talents (Matt. 25:14–30) shows, Christians will be held accountable for the way in which we manage God's affairs as stewards. Let's explore this parable in detail.

For the kingdom of heaven is as a man travelling into a far country, who called his own servants, and delivered unto them his goods. And unto one he gave five talents, to another two, and to another one; to every man according to his several ability; and straightway took his journey. Then he that had received the five talents went and traded with the same, and made them other five talents. And likewise he that had received two, he also gained other two. But he that had received one went and digged in the earth, and hid his lord's money. After a long time the lord of those servants cometh, and reckoneth with them. And so he that had received five talents came and brought other five talents, saying, Lord, thou deliveredst unto me five talents: behold, I have gained beside them five talents more. His lord said unto him, Well done, thou good and faithful servant: thou hast been faithful over a few things, I will make thee ruler over many things: enter thou into the joy of thy lord. He also that had received two talents came and said, Lord, thou deliveredst unto me two talents: behold, I have gained two other talents beside them. His lord said unto him, Well done, good and faithful servant; thou hast been faithful over a few things, I will make thee ruler over many things: enter thou into the joy of thy lord. Then he which had received the one talent came and said, Lord, I knew thee that thou art an hard man, reaping where thou hast not sown, and gathering where thou hast not strawed: And I was afraid, and went and hid thy talent in the earth: lo, there thou hast that is thine. His lord answered and said unto him, Thou wicked and slothful servant, thou knewest that I reap where I sowed not, and gather where I have not strawed: Thou oughtest therefore to have put my money to the exchangers, and then at my coming I should have received mine own with usury. Take therefore the talent from him, and give it unto him which hath ten talents. For unto every one that hath shall be given, and he shall have abundance: but from him that hath not shall be taken away even that which he hath. And cast ye the unprofitable servant into outer darkness: there shall be weeping and gnashing of teeth.

Lack of Knowledge

In this parable, the interaction between the master and the stewards is representative of the kingdom of heaven. The master gave the servants HIS goods. The goods can be interpreted as spiritual goods or earthly goods. We will focus on the value of the goods in terms of them being material possessions. He gave them each a different portion of his goods. He gave them the portion according to his right or sovereignty to do so. Each servant then made a decision about what to do with the money that was given to him. The master did not provide any instructions on what to do with the money, he simply gave it to them. Two of them traded what was given to him and earned interest on the money. One of them decided not to do anything with the money, but hide it. Our Master has given us talents as well. We too have to make a decision as to what we are going to do with it. The mindset of the two who traded their money was obviously one of responsibility. They knew that they had a responsibility to manage the master's money wisely. They realized that the money did not belong to them and also that there would come a time when they would have to give an account to their master for the money. They fully understood the role of a steward. Verse 19 says that at some point in the future the master returned to inquire as to the state of his finances that he gave to them. His inquiry implies that he had an expectation of something when he returned. The parable goes on to say that the master was very pleased with the return on his investment provided by the two servants. He was so pleased at their faithfulness that he would make them ruler of many other things. In other words, he was pleased to see how diligent and careful they were with their respective talents, he knew that he could trust them with even more. **As stewards for God's finances, He fully expects to hold us accountable for how we use His assets.** We will have to give an account for it.

The master was very disappointed that the one servant did not manage his money wisely. Notice that he did not spend it foolishly or use it for evil, he simply hid it. God referred to the servant as wicked and slothful due to the lack of managing the money. God views us as lazy and evil when we don't manage the things that He has given unto us wisely. Proverbs 18:9 says *"He also that is slothful in his work is brother to him that is a great waster"*. Being slothful is the same thing as being wasteful!!! A lesson for us is to be aware **that not doing anything with what God has given to us is just as bad as mismanaging it.** The trap that the enemy designed is for us to think that as long as we're not being careless with our finances, we are not displeasing God or that is all that He expects. Isn't it interesting that the one that probably had to exert the least effort in trading his talent didn't apply any effort? He only had one talent to work with. He didn't have to think about diversification, he simply had to make the best of it. This happens with Christians all the time. The people with the largest amount of free time to dedicate to ministry, the least financial strain or the greatest talent to offer tend to bury it. For example, let's pretend that you are not struggling with the issue of debt, most assets are paid off and you are able to save and/or invest a substantial amount of money each month. You offer only the tithe monthly to God. Compare that to someone who is struggling financially and have very little spare time to dedicate to ministry. It seems that the latter person somehow manages to give offerings and to other ministries above the tithe and is often the first to volunteer to support ministry efforts.

Let's look deeper at the mindset of the one who had the one talent. Pay attention to his logic or rationale and relate it to your current thinking. He offered excuses *first*. Isn't it very interesting that he offered excuses before he even gave the account? Verses 24-25—He claims great familiarity with the master as a hard man and claims that he was afraid of him because of this. In fact he really did not know him at all because he did not anticipate the day of reckoning. He actually contradicted himself—he claimed that he was so familiar with him that he was afraid of him, yet he did not know him well enough to know the master's expectation when he returned. If he really knew the master, he would have fully expected that the master would be looking for a return on his investment. So often this is the case with us. We claim to know and love God, yet our actions indicate that we don't know Him at all. To know Him is to love Him. To love Him is to be aware of His character and his expectations. To have this awareness leads to diligent efforts to meet those expectations. We say things like "God has not made a way for me to get out of this financial bondage yet, so I'm just going to maintain the pace until He does" or "I know God is going to deliver me from this debt in the next few weeks." So you do nothing. This sound very good and spiritual, but is the wrong attitude to have. If you really knew Him, you would know that it is not His will that you remain in financial bondage. You would begin to diligently do the things that would improve the situation. **He will supply the wisdom and direction because He loves us, but we have to do the work.** The servant's incorrect knowledge and assumptions about the master led to unhealthy fear and resulted in inactivity. When we don't truly know our Master, we fall into the trap of fearing only the wrath of God and that causes us to do nothing. In verse 25 the servant says *"Lo, there thou hast that is thine"*—I have given you back what you have given to me. He is saying that you have at least received back what you gave to me. I didn't waste what you gave to me. He totally missed the responsibility and accountability of stewardship lesson. His attitude obviously was that he wanted to keep what the master gave to him—not increase at all, definitely not decrease, just maintain. He hid the master's talent—"I kept it safe". He felt he did good because at least he kept the money in a bank or safe place. The others kept it safe too, just in interest-bearing accounts, mutual funds and other "safe" investments. As you can see the differences are subtle, yet powerful and impactful. The sad thing is that the servant really felt that he was justified in his actions.

The Consequences

Another very important lesson in this parable is that there are consequences for our actions. The excuse that he gave was illogical. The master responded in effect by saying, "If you knew that I reap where I have not sown you should have known that I would come looking for a return and should have traded what I gave you. You should have expected to give me to usury—or interest". The result of the mismanagement is that the one talent that he was given was taken away and given to the other wise servants. If you don't wisely manage what you are given, at some point, God may take the little that you think you have away and give it to someone that has proven themselves to be faithful over God's finances. Have you ever seen someone that seems to continue to receive financial blessings on a regular basis? That may very well be the consequence of their faithfulness in stewardship. The servant is then labeled as unprofitable and then cast into outer darkness. This represents being put in a place where there are miseries, darkness, no joy and active and persistent attacks. When we are not faithful stewards by God's definition of stewardship, we open ourselves up to very negative consequences that could compound. In other words, when we are not acting as faithful stewards, the situation ends up getting worse. We begin to feel like we're in a financial pit with no light in sight. That is the reward of unfaithfulness.

When you fully comprehend that you are steward, not an owner, it will change your perspective on many things in life. You realize that you have a responsibility, will be held accountable and that there are consequences. With these in mind, each purchasing decision takes on a different focus and meaning. Your internal dialogue changes from "what should I buy with this extra money?" to "God, what would you like for me to buy with your extra money?". You then consider whether each purchase is a wise decision. You begin to have in the front of your mind that you are going to be held accountable for the decision that you make. A revelation that you should have by now is **that God does not own or desire only the tenth or tithe, but He owns 100%. His expectation is that you are being diligent and faithful with all of your money.** Knowing this should aid in lifting all financial burdens. You are being asked to manage money for an all-knowing and all-powerful God!!! Since it is His money, it's in good hands. Why not seek His counsel on how to manage your finances? Knowing this also makes the loss of material things less burdensome. If you truly followed the leading of God when purchasing that item, and it is destroyed, then God lost it not you. Get this in your spirit!! Transfer the title to every item in your possession to God right now. Commit to a renewed attitude about money and possessions. In a later chapter I will provide tips on using the tool designed to track your account-ability—a budget.

❏ **Complete Gaining and Maintaining the Proper Perspective worksheet.**

CHAPTER 3
TITHES AND OFFERINGS

It is very rare to hear messages from the pulpit about tithes and offerings as the main sermon. Any comment on the subject is limited to the time set aside during the service for giving tithes and offerings. At this time, we typically here Malachi 3:8-11—*Will a man rob God? Yet ye have robbed me. But ye say, Wherein have we robbed thee? In tithes and offerings. Ye are cursed with a curse: for ye have robbed me, even this whole nation. Bring ye all the tithes into the storehouse, that there may be meat in mine house, and prove me now herewith, saith the LORD of hosts, if I will not open you the windows of heaven, and pour you out a blessing, that there shall not be room enough to receive it. And I will rebuke the devourer for your sakes, and he shall not destroy the fruits of your ground; neither shall your vine cast her fruit before the time in the field, saith the LORD of hosts.* In my experience, it was rare for the speaker to elaborate on this scripture. If any insights were offered, it was specifically geared toward making you feel guilty for not tithing. Sometimes the emphasis was placed on the blessing that would come from God if you did tithe. Either way, the message focused on tithing so that you don't feel bad about robbing God or to receive blessings as the only motivation. The conclusion that I drew for most of my Christian life was that if I gave God 10% and some offerings, then I would receive bountiful blessings from Him. In some ways, this became my true motive for giving. I would venture to say that I am not the only one who had this motive. These weren't necessarily wrong motives, but my heart wasn't truly in it. If many Christians were to be honest with themselves, they would admit the true motives. First, let's take a close look at these scriptures in the context in which it was written.

Verse 8—*Will a man rob God? Yet ye have robbed me. But ye say, Wherein have we robbed thee? In tithes and offerings.* In the book of Malachi, the prophet gives very stern rebuke to Israel. In verse 7 of this chapter, God recalls how Israel has frequently turned away from His statutes. He asks them to return to Him. The people ask Malachi how they should come back to God. Here in verse 8, God gives a very specific example of the sin that has caused their current state. He refers to their disobedience as robbery. Really think about this. He is saying that we, His creation, have robbed the very Creator! The people responded in a very human way. They basically were wondering how could they be accused of robbing someone that they love. They wanted to know "How could we possibly rob You, God?" God responded quickly with the specifics of the theft—tithes and offerings.

The tithe in the Old Testament was required out of simple obedience to God. The tithe means tenth. There were actually three tithes required of Israel. One was for the priests and Levites (Numbers 18:21,24), one for a specific festival and the last one supported the poor, widows and strangers in need in their community. These can be found in Deuteronomy 14:22-29. The tithes offered for the Levites and the festival were required regularly. The tithe for the community was required every three years. To tithe was to agree with the law of God and His sovereignty. Tithing was an acknowledgment that God is the owner of everything. The offerings in Israel were the firstfruits. This was the first of ripe fruit, grains and other harvest. To give the firstfruits was to give God the best. It is both the best and the first. The tithe and offerings were material things that were given to God that represented a spiritual matter, obedience. The principle remains that of giving to God in honor of who He is. In summary, to rob God here meant to rob Him of the honor that was due to Him and the acknowledgment of his sovereignty. The medium set aside to do this was the tithe and offerings. It has nothing to do with the money, per se. It has everything to do with obedience and putting Him first. Remember that it is His already!

Verse 9—*Ye are cursed with a curse: for ye have robbed me, even this whole nation.* The consequence of robbing God is the current curse they were under. At the time there was a famine in the land. In effect, denying God what was due to Him resulted in withdrawal of holding back of their blessings. I believe that this is really where their earlier question was coming from. When they emphatically asked, "wherein have we robbed thee?" I believe the motive was not so much out of ignorance than it was self-defense. Due to the lack they were experiencing in the land, they could not see how they could possibly be accused of robbing God when they had nothing to show for it. Surely if they had in fact robbed Almighty God they would have many riches to show for it. Now with their current state, they would use the excuse that they did not have anything to give. Without a harvest, how could they possibly give the firstfruits or the tithe? They missed the entire relationship that their giving had on their current state. The cause and effect relationship was not apparent to them at the time, but God made it very clear to them. They had the famine <u>because</u> of their disobedience in giving the tithe and offerings. Many Christians today misunderstand or are ignorant of this very important relationship between giving and receiving and obedience. We often say things like:

- I will tithe after I get rid of some of these bills.
- God would want me to get out of debt first and then tithe *(this topic is addressed later)*
- I can't afford to tithe
- God knows my heart (How true this is!!)

We never stop to think that we may be in the financial stress that we are in because we don't honor God in our giving. Not honoring God has caused the curse to be placed on us. The very thing that was intended to bless them now caused or contributed to their downfall. Now let's see how God instructed them to reverse the curse.

Verse 10—*Bring ye all the tithes into the storehouse, that there may be meat in mine house, and prove me now herewith, saith the LORD of hosts, if I will not open you the windows of heaven, and pour you out a blessing, that there shall not be room enough to receive it.*

Action and obedience are required to reverse the curse. God didn't change the law because of their disobedience. He simply restated the law that was given—bring all the tithes. This is very important. Very often, we expect God to change the rules of engagement for us. He is faithful to His Word. **He will not deviate from what He has already said, but He is so good, that He will gladly repeat it for us to make sure that we get it.** Emphasis is placed on *all*. Perhaps some were bringing a portion of the tithe, still robbing God. The storehouse was the inner chamber which was a physical location in the temple where the offerings were gathered. The reason the tithe was to be brought was so that there would be food in God's house. This was primarily for the care of the Levites. I believe that it is appropriate to relate the storehouse to the local church of today since this is the place where believers fellowship and congregate just as they did at the temple at the time of this writing. Here God invites the people to take Him up on His word. This is fascinating to me! Almighty God who is sovereign invites His people to put Him to the test. Prior to Malachi, the people of Israel had numerous experiences with Him and could surely testify to His faithfulness toward them. God had already outlined the results of obeying His commands in Deuteronomy 28 and I'm sure the people with Malachi knew of these promises. God so kindly offers the people to test Him. It should have been enough for God to simply command or instruct them to bring the tithes to the storehouse. Because of His love for the people He gives them what I believe to be that extra assurance that He will perform His Word for them. He recognized their current state of famine and realized that it would be a hard thing for them to fathom bringing in the tithes and offering when they had so little themselves. The offer to prove Him is an awesome example of how God will provide us with the extra assurance we need to have faith in Him.

He then gives them a glimpse of what to expect if they do. He says that He would empty out a blessing from heaven on them. The phrase "windows of heaven" was also used in Genesis 7:11 in reference to the flood. It reads *In the six hundredth year of Noah's life, in the second month, the seventeenth day of the month, the same day were all the fountains of the great deep broken up, and the windows of heaven were opened.* This phrase refers to a constant, long term deluge. **The type of blessing promised by God is one that is constant, with a lot of power, long term, seemingly never ending and it looks like more than you can handle.** When God opened the windows of heaven in the days of Noah, the earth could barely contain the water. It lasted until God said it was enough. Man could not control the downpour nor avoid it. The type of blessing that God will unleash will overtake you. It is the type of blessing that you cannot avoid benefiting from if you tried. It is a powerful blessing. I'm sure that the people of Israel thought that Malachi was not hearing from God on this one because it did not sound logical. He was telling them that God said to give out of the little that you have and I will bless you bountifully. What seemed logical to them was for God to remove the famine, restore the harvest and they would then resume giving the tithe and offering. We too think like the children of Israel on this subject—"Surely God would not expect me to give out of the little that I have because I can barely make ends meet now" or "I will give once I get on my feet". We spend so much time in prayer and at the altar asking for financial blessings when the key to it is in our own hand, we just choose not to use it. I believe this is one of the most deadly traps that the enemy has planted for us. He knows that following this principle works, but he wants us ignorant to it. Giving is a matter of faith and trust. God offers a challenge in this scripture to prove Him despite our logic. Numbers 23:19 confirms that God will make good on His challenge to us—*God is not a man, that he should lie; neither the son of man, that he should repent: hath he said, and shall he not do it? or hath he spoken, and shall he not make it good?* You have nothing to lose!!!

Verse 11—*And I will rebuke the devourer for your sakes, and he shall not destroy the fruits of your ground; neither shall your vine cast her fruit before the time in the field, saith the LORD of hosts.* God also promises to aggressively fight off anything that seeks to destroy or consume their harvest. He will keep a watchful eye over their well being. In other words, God will make sure that those things that can consume or destroy your harvest are eliminated.

After studying these scriptures several things should stick with you:

- The principle that is being discussed is giving.
- The tithe and offering were the specific types of giving mandated by God in the law
- Abiding by the law of tithes and offerings was a way of demonstrating obedience to God
- Robbing God of tithes and offerings mean to deny Him of the honor that is due Him and His sovereignty
- The storehouse is an inner chamber in the temple where the tithes and offerings were gathered
- God expects us to give out of whatever we have—little or much.
- To return to the state of the harvest, give the tithe and offering to God
- This restoration is guaranteed to trigger an outpouring of a phenomenal blessing from God
- As a part of the restoration, God will make sure that the enemy does not consume or devour the blessings.

Tithing and the New Testament

A very important fact that is also rarely discussed is that there is no reference to the principle of tithing in terms of a command in the New Testament. Jesus did refer to the tithe in Matthew 23:23 in His condemnation of the Pharisees. He said *Woe unto you, scribes and Pharisees, hypocrites! for ye pay tithe of mint and anise and cummin, and have omitted the weightier matters of the law, judgment, mercy, and faith: these ought ye to have done, and not to leave the other undone.* He says that they have paid their tithe as they should have. It was their duty under the Mosaic law to do this. He however calls them hypocrites because they were religious in their duty to pay the tithe, but neglected the spirit of the law regarding giving. They appeared holy on the outside for paying the tithe. He says the more important things of law, judgment, mercy and faith were left out. These are all things that reflect the internal motives of man—his heart. Jesus says, that these things are more important and carry more weight than just paying the tithe out of duty. This is a tremendous lesson and warning for us. We become hypocrites when we give the tithe only as a matter of religion, but neglect to do the spiritual things that are expressions of our heart. There is some debate about whether tithing should even be discussed in the church today. Many say that tithing is legalism and we are living under grace now. I believe that just because tithing is not specifically mentioned does not mean the spirit behind tithing is irrelevant for the Church today. I do however believe that it is the motive or spirit behind the principle of tithing that is misunderstood. Jesus said Himself *"Think not that I am come to destroy the law, or the prophets: I am not come to destroy, but to fulfil"* (Matthew 5:17). He came to make real and plain the spiritual intent of the law. In many of the laws of the Old Testament, God was really after the heart of the matter. His covenant with His people attempted to drive the heart through the law. Jesus came to demonstrate the heart of the matter. He said that He came to fulfill the law (Scripture). In other words, He came to demonstrate and show us the spirit of the law. Tithing was the law, there was a spiritual behavior that the law was attempting to spark. I believe that **we see the same principle given and fulfilled in the New Testament regarding tithing, it is just addressed through the principle of giving. Tithing is a form of giving.** Hebrews Chapter 8 speaks of the superiority of the new covenant. It is superior because the Word is now in our hearts and no longer do we need the law to structure our activities. In the next chapter we will examine some of the New Testament scriptures on giving.

CHAPTER 4

GIVING

In this chapter we will examine giving according to the Old and New Testament. Keep in mind that giving involves more than money. We are able to give our time, our counsel, things, or talents. For the purpose of this study, we will relate the principles to giving money. Recall that paying the tithe was done out of obedience in the Old Testament. It didn't require much thought or emotion because it was a requirement to pay the tithe. It was paid to serve as a reminder that God owned everything. Even if someone did not want to pay the tithe, they paid it out of obedience. Voluntary offerings are also mentioned in the Old Testament. These types of offerings required a response of the heart. A person had to decide to give beyond the tithe because they desired to give. It was not based on a requirement of the law. These freewill offerings are mentioned in Leviticus 22, Numbers 15 and Exodus 35.

In Exodus 35, God instructed Moses to ask the people to bring an offering to complete the work on the tabernacle. It reads *Take ye from among you an offering unto the LORD: whosoever is of a willing heart, let him bring it, an offering of the LORD; gold, and silver, and brass....* The condition of the heart of the giver is emphasized here. God didn't just ask for the people to give. He specifically said those "of a willing heart" are to bring their offering. I believe that the acceptance of the offering is contingent upon the heart of the giver. We will examine this closer later in this chapter when we explore 2 Corinthians 9. The response of the people is simply awesome and a good example for us today. This can be found in verses 20-21—*And all the congregation of the children of Israel departed from the presence of Moses. And they came, every one whose heart stirred him up, and every one whom his spirit made willing, and they brought the LORD's offering to the work of the tabernacle of the congregation, and for all his service, and for the holy garments.* Again, emphasis is placed on the heart of the giver. Those that had a willing heart responded <u>immediately</u>. They were responding to God, not Moses. I believe this is where many of us miss the blessing today. **We believe or act as if our giving is in response to the man or woman of God rather than obedience to God. We often take so much time to analyze the request and examine the words used in the appeal to give that we miss God in it totally!** The Israelites immediately recognized that this request was from God through Moses. They therefore responded immediately to God's request. They were not promised anything in return for their giving. This was not a motive for their giving. The bible says that *every one whose heart stirred him up, and every one whom his spirit made willing,* gave an offering. Let's look closer at their attitude of giving and the significance of their immediate response.

There were various types of items that the people gave as offerings. They offered bracelets, earring, rings, jewels, fine linen, goat's hair, silver and brass just to name a few. These valuable items were a part of the spoil that the Israelites took from Egypt when they departed. They could have very easily assumed that since God had allowed them to have these fine and expensive things, surely He would not expect to get them back as an offering. He would expect for them to enjoy those gifts. The children of Israel had exactly the opposite attitude toward those things. They brought those same blessings and offered them willingly to God. Their willingness points directly to their priorities and reverence for God. They obviously kept the "things" in perspective. They recognized that it all belonged to God anyway. They were not bound by the things and were quick to depart from them to express their love and thanks to God. Think about the times you have been asked or prompted to give. Did you have to think long and hard about what to give or how much to give? Or did you respond immediately because your heart was fixed on pleasing God? Did you automatically exclude certain things or a certain amount from even being considered in giving? Did you just give what you had in your pocket at the time so that you can say that you gave something? Or did you do like the

Israelites and depart and return immediately with offerings in hand? Sometimes we say that we have to pray about how much or what to give. I think that this is definitely in order in many cases. However, in some cases, I believe we use this as a stalling tactic or excuse not to give. When it comes to a willing offering, it is up to you in your heart to *decide*. The instruction was for those that had a willing heart to give. You can pray about it, but in the end, you still must be willing to give.

Another important fact to note is that everyone gave, even the children (verse 29). Too many times we exclude the children from giving. We need to realize that children can have a willing heart also. It is good for them to participate in giving to God at an early age. The Israelites didn't just give their offering one time, they continued to give. In chapter 36, verse 3, the bible says ...*and they brought yet unto him free offerings every morning!* Note that Moses did NOT make another appeal each morning, yet the people continued to give daily. Today the very opposite happens when funding the kingdom business is at hand. We give the one time offering and expect that it will be sufficient. In fact, we get upset if another appeal is made because we think that the person is being greedy or out of order. The preacher has to continue to provide financial updates to encourage the people to give more until the goal is met. The fact that they gave each morning speaks to the priority they placed on giving. It also speaks to the joy they must have had to give. What a lesson for us to learn. Randy Alcorn summarized the giving of the Israelites this way:

> No one ever had to say, "I feel led to tithe," or ask, "Would you like me to give the firstfruits, Lord?' The answer had already been given in Scripture. Voluntary giving started after the firstfruits. The tithe was never a ceiling for giving, only a floor. It was a beginning point. Beyond it, God's children gave more, some-times much more, as needs and opportunities arose.

The people gave so much that Moses had to command the people to stop giving. *And Moses gave commandment, and they caused it to be proclaimed throughout the camp, saying, Let neither man nor woman make any more work for the offering of the sanctuary. So the people were restrained from bringing. For the stuff they had was sufficient for all the work to make it, and too much* (Exodus 36:6-7). Keep in mind that this was above and beyond the tithe. Tithes and offerings are both forms of giving.

First and foremost, it is an expectation that Christians give. Let's look at 2nd Corinthians 9:6-7 *But this I say, He which soweth sparingly shall reap also sparingly; and he which soweth bountifully shall reap also bountifully. 7Every man according as he purposeth in his heart, so let him give; not grudgingly, or of necessity: for God loveth a cheerful giver.* I recall hearing this scripture quite frequently during the time set aside for giving. Again, rarely did I hear anyone expound on it. When I did, it was primarily to emphasize the cheerful giving aspect. Very often we hear the speaker say "Let's stay in the spirit of worship and continue to worship God in our giving". I find it interesting that we have to remind Christians that giving to God is a form of worship and not to be taken lightly. I'm glad we do make the statement as a reminder. I believe that this is primarily due to the fact that we do not fully comprehend the spiritual principles of giving and what God is really trying to achieve in our giving. If we truly understood this, then we would have our checks written out before we get to church or our cash in hand or already set aside. If we understood giving principles, we would not use the time designated to collect the offering to use the bathroom. We would reverence this time. In this scripture, Paul is reminding them of the importance of having their offering ready when the brethren arrive at Corinth to minister to them. This reminder implies that there had been an occasion when they were not prepared. Keep in mind that the Christians that he was addressing were in extreme poverty at the time—*How that in a great trial of affliction the abundance of their joy and their deep poverty abounded unto the riches of their liberality* (2nd Corinthians 8:2). In verse 6, Paul takes the opportunity to also remind them of this powerful principle of giving. In other words, "while I'm on this topic, let me remind you of the expectation when it comes to giving". In these two short verses, he addresses the benefits of giving, the consequences of not giving and how to give. More importantly he addresses what God expects from the giver. He begins by stating that there is a definite relationship between how much you sow and what you can expect to reap. The return that you receive is directly determined by your investment. Solomon also had something to say about this in Proverbs 11:24—*There is he that generously scatter abroad, and yet increase more; there are those who withold more than is fitting or what is justly due, but it results only in want.* Take the time to read this Proverb again. It is saying that those that generously give somehow end up receiving more. Conversely, those that do not give that which they should find themselves in want. This does not agree with human logic at all. The more you give, the more you have and the less you give, the less you have. Many of us apply our own logic to our tithes and offering. We say that we just don't have it to give. While that may in fact be a true statement in terms of not having the money to give at that moment, we must realize the principle that we are employing when we continue to use this as an excuse. You don't have anything to give, because you are not a habitual giver. You find yourself in want because you don't give. You have not included yourself in the giving cycle. Read the Proverb again until you get it in your spirit!!! Break the cycle and just determine to give!!! This principle works for whomever uses it. It definitely requires faith to begin operating according to this principle. But isn't that true with everything in our spiritual walk with God? Somehow, we think that faith is not required in our finances. I believe this is because of our perspective on money and the fact that it is tangible. We believe that it takes faith to get the healing that we request. In cases of healing, we often confuse faith and hope. We want it so bad, that we feel we don't have a choice but to believe God. With our finances, we think that we do have choices because it is our money. We don't even conceive of activating faith in our financial decisions, especially in our giving. We must begin to exercise faith in giving.

Jesus also addressed the benefits of giving. In Luke 6:38—*Give, and it shall be given unto you; good measure, pressed down, and shaken together, and running over, shall men give into your bosom. For with the same measure that ye mete withal it shall be measured to you again.* I remember a song that we used to sing during the offering time that said "You can't beat God giving, no matter how you try. The more you give, the more He gives to you…". That is exactly what this verse is saying. When you give, God will make sure that He returns the generosity toward you over and above what you gave. Whatever the amount is, that will be used to measure what comes back to you. Again, regardless of the amount you give, it will return to you in good measure. It is pressed down to make room for more and it will still run over. Remember this is Jesus talking here. This is a guaranteed return on your investment!!! Let's return to 2nd Corinthians—next in verse 7, Paul says that giving is a personal thing and a matter of the heart. This is something that you decide to do. He did not state a minimum or maximum amount that is expected. A percentage is also not mentioned. For those that limit their giving to the tithe or 10%, they are falling significantly short of the expectation. Their giving is solely based on what they have decided to give. Next he says that your attitude behind your giving is important—*…not grudgingly, or of necessity.* Based on this scripture it is possible to make up your mind about how much you are going to give, but have the wrong attitude about giving it. For example, you can decide to give $200 in the offering. But your motive for giving can be because that is the amount that was requested from the pulpit. I believe that grudgingly can be applied to the giving of tithes. This goes back to the law of tithing. If you decide to give the $200 because it is 10% and you have been taught to tithe, but you really want to use that money for something else, then that is considering giving grudgingly. Any attitude of hostility, resentment or spite falls into the category of grudgingly. I have done this. I have been in church where a speaker has requested a certain dollar amount from each person in the congregation. In fact, he asked those that could give $100 to come forward, then those that could give $50 stand. Then he said for those that were sitting to pray about their giving. He then began to talk about how the money that we were holding on to was going to be spent somewhere else anyway and it would be better if we planted it in the kingdom. He then proceeded to make us feel bad for not giving at least $40 dollars. Then he asked the ones that were giving the $100 or $50 to place their money in a particular basket. He then asked those that could give $40 to stand. He continued until he got down to $25. He then lumped everyone else together and asked them to bring forth their offering. With each round of his asking, he interjected his thoughts on making the sacrifice to give in this particular offering. Now this was our normal time set aside for giving. This was not a special occasion, but this was a guest speaker. I gave $40, but I had an attitude of resentment and definite hostility. Because of my role in this particular church I did not want to be seen as giving "with the others" that were lumped together in the under $25 offering. So you see, I gave, but it was grudgingly. I'm sure that I was not the only one. So, how do you think that offering was received by God? I'm sure that the amount raised at that service exceeded the average Sunday offering, but how did God view it? He concludes verse 7 with what pleases God—a cheerful giver. In other words, God is pleased and loves it when we give out of a sincere heart and willing desire to do it. There should be excitement and a great desire present when we give. Remember that Paul did not indicate an amount here because the focus is on the act of giving and the attitude in which it is given.

Give Regularly

In 1st Corinthians 16:2 Paul talks about additional aspects of giving—*Upon the first day of the week let every one of you lay by him in store, as God hath prospered him, that there be no gatherings when I come.* In giving, the requirement is that it is regular, everyone participates and it should be proportionate to how God has blessed you. Giving should be planned and occur regularly. This is what is meant by "having a mind to give". When you have a mind to give, you make plans and develop strategies, if necessary, to give. We should always have a mind to give. Just like we plan to make a trip to the grocery store or plan to go to bed at a specific time to get some rest, we should plan to give. The New Testament makes no reference at all to giving 10% as the only requirement. In the context of this scripture, even if you gave 10%, you could still be robbing God. Look at it again. The giving is to *be "as God hath prospereth him"*. So, as you can see, in some cases, it should be greater than the 10%. It should be proportionate to your blessing. If Christians planned to give then we would not see the pressure that we see today being applied from the pulpit for money. If giving were systematic and planned, then church budgeting would be much easier and there would be less need to call special meetings to meet a need. It would also be unnecessary to prolong the giving time by making repeated appeals for more money. Can you see how God intended for His people to fund kingdom business? When we plan to give and give with the right attitude, the church can have greater confidence in its budgeting process and make plans with assurance that the funds will be there. When giving is seasonal or sporadic, the church has to move slower in executing its plans because the funds are unpredictable.

Result of Giving

And God is able to make all grace abound toward you; that ye, always having all sufficiency in all things, may abound to every good work: (2nd Corinthians 9:8). Paul tells them that by being obedient and willing to give to God first, their earthly needs will be met. This verse in the Amplified Bible reads

> *"And God is able to make all grace (every favor and earthly blessing) come to you in abundance, so that you may always and under all circumstances and whatever the need be self-*sufficient [possessing enough to require no aid or support and furnished in abundance for every good work and charitable donation].

Giving the right way will result in spiritual and material blessings. I was so blessed by this scripture because it says that all of my needs will be met under all circumstances. Even if the economy is bad, I'll have what I need. Even in the midst of layoffs, I will have what I need. Not only will I have my needs met, they will be met with abundance. This is the blessing that God can impart when you give according to the scripture. This is the same thing that Jesus said in Matthew 6:33—*But seek ye first the kingdom of God, and his righteousness; and all these things shall be added unto you.*

Giving and Increase

In verse 10, Paul states what God will do for them as a result of their giving. It can also be read as a prayer that Paul is praying for their increase. *Now he that ministereth seed to the sower both minister bread for your food, and multiply your seed sown, and increase the fruits of your righteousness*; He that ministereth seed to the sower is God. Paul is referring to God meeting the material needs of the giver. He also says that the seed sown will be multiplied. Many times today, we hear the heart of this same prayer during the time of offering in church. The request is that God will multiply the amount that was given so that more good can be accomplished with the offering. Paul also says that the fruit of their right attitude and obedience in giving will be increase. Increase is a by-product of giving.

The Purpose of Increase

> *Being enriched in every thing to all bountifulness, which causeth through us thanksgiving to God. For the administration of this service not only supplieth the want of the saints, but is abundant also by many thanksgivings unto God; Whiles by the experiment of this ministration they glorify God for your professed subjection unto the gospel of Christ, and for your liberal distribution unto them, and unto all men*

Paul then tells them in verse 11 what to do with a portion of the increase. *Thus you will be enriched in all things and in every way, so that you can be generous, and [your generosity as it is] adminis-*

tered by us will bring forth thanksgiving to God (Amplified Bible). They are being blessed with the material and spiritual blessings so that they can continue to give. He then says that because of your generosity, others will break out with thanksgiving to God. The recipients of the seed sown will attribute their blessings to God and begin to give Him thanks. We really need to understand why we are so richly blessed. We are not supposed to hold on to everything that we have and just call it a wonderful blessing. We are told in this scripture that we are to give even more when we are blessed.

The ultimate purpose of this generous giving is to glorify God (verse 13). God is glorified when we give generously because the recipients and others will see that their needs are being met and give God the glory for it. Paul also mentions the purpose of the abundance in 2nd Corinthians 8:13-*14—For I mean not that other men be eased, and ye burdened: But by an equality, that now at this time your abundance may be a supply for their want, that their abundance also may be a supply for your want: that there may be equality.* God definitely has a plan to meet the needs of His people. Paul says that the abundance of money or things that you have is intended to meet the needs of those that have less. We are to bring about the financial balance in church. We should be able to assist the body of Christ with their debt reduction plans. We should be able to go to the church when there is a need and expect to have the need met without causing a financial strain on the church. Let's bring this closer to home. Giving is not limited to the money we give to the church. We should apply these principles to other forms of giving as well. We should plan to give help to those in need and do it regularly. We should have the right attitude in this giving. We should expect that we will have our needs met when we do this.

The cycle of giving should be evident after reading this chapter.

- God supplies the needs and abundance to His people
- Out of thanksgiving and obedience to God, His people give generously
- Giving results in material needs being met
- Giving results in abundant blessings
- You are able to give more out of your abundance

- You are able to assist in meeting the needs of others
- Through your giving others give thanks to God
- God is glorified!!!

❏ **Complete the Renewed Thinking—Giving worksheet.**

CHAPTER 5
TRUTH IN SPENDING

There are many scriptures in the Bible related to money. The principle in each passage is not money itself, but the attitudes and actions that are attached to the money and possessions. Christians are ignorant about their finances and biblical principles concerning them primarily because we don't realize that the money does not belong to us. We believe that how we spend the money is not something that God has to or wants to be involved in. Since our leaders do not proactively teach on personal finances from the biblical perspective we naturally assume that it is not a spiritual issue or related to our spiritual growth. For some reason we have DECIDED that financial advice from the Bible is not for "today". With this mentality, we end up spending without thought or purpose. We spend to meet whatever physical, material or emotional need that we have. The result is uncontrolled spending that leads to a downward spiral and many negative consequences. We end up spending instead of giving. Doing this places us in a different cycle that produces very different results from the giving cycle. The objective of this chapter is to explore spending habits and uncover the deeply rooted beliefs that are resulting in the current financial situation. You must commit to being completely honest with yourself. It will take prayer and honesty to successfully turn this area of your life around. One reason for this is that habits are truly hard to break. When we have developed certain habits, we tend to exclude them from scrutiny. It is time to come face to face with those areas.

Where is the money going?

This is a question that we often ask ourselves. Unfortunately, we ask it as a rhetorical question and never take the time to actually answer the question. We will discuss later how to determine where the money is going before constructing a budget. At that point the question will be answered with facts. Now, I want to focus on answering the question "Why is the money going there". This question has to be answered from the heart. Your heart is hidden from man, so no one can accurately answer this question except you. A financial counselor cannot answer this question for you. The reason you need to be able to respond to this question honestly is because it will identify the root or source of your financial dilemma. Too often, we embark on building a budget but we never address the source of our problems. We end up building in these issues into the budget and do not succeed in meeting our financial goals. Why we spend money on certain things and why we feel we must have certain things must be addressed so that we accurately and wisely eliminate unnecessary items from our spending. When reviewing our spending habits, we have to look at why we are spending. There is a decision that is made with each purchase. The decision may be well thought out or simply made impulsively. In either case, there is a motive behind the decision to spend each dollar that is spent. The decision may not necessarily be made based on the amount of the item but is often based on the item itself. The item may have social status, financial security, wealth, class, pride or esteem attached to it in your mind. So when you make a purchase, you in fact are *buying* status, pride, self esteem, etc. The item becomes the secondary thing. We are purchasing the perception that it creates in many cases. Because that perception is so important to us, we do not give much thought to how we get it or if we can afford it. At the moment, we just want the feeling it gives or the perception it creates.

Why Buy It?

Every purchase that we make has a spiritual impact or consequence if you search out the motives behind the purchase. Think about the last 2 purchases that you made that exceeded $100 per item. Ask yourself the following questions:

- why the purchase was made
- was it a necessity
- did you charge it or pay cash
- did you have to have it at the time you bought it
- why did you choose that particular brand
- Did you pray about the purchase

Answering these questions will uncover the true motive for the purchase. Let's assume that you purchased a digital camera. Let's assume the following answers for the questions:

- The camera was purchased in order to be able to take digital pictures
- It was not a necessity. You currently have 2 other cameras that work
- Charged the purchased to Best Buy card
- Did not need it at the time
- Chose the brand because of recommendation of the salesperson
- You did not pray about the purchase.

If we assess the answers, we could conclude that the digital camera was purchased simply because you wanted to have one. So what could possibly be the spiritual impact of this purchase?

- Charging the purchase leads to increase in debt. This may lead to more anxiety, which competes with worship and praise.

- Less money to save or give. There are incremental expenditures that will creep in (film for the camera, processing costs of digital pictures, batteries) that have to be considered.
- Transferred reliance from God to self. The danger of self sufficiency robs us of valuable insight and wisdom of the will of God for our lives.

Now you may be thinking that purchasing a digital camera is not going to have this deep spiritual impact. Well it absolutely can. We tend not to think beyond the item though. Think about your recent purchases again. Do you have any anxiety over making the payments? Does it require more of your time to maintain the item? If so, this is time that is taken away from family or the things of God. I must reiterate that the issue is not with the item(s) that was purchased. The problem is with the money spent, the energy exerted, the enthusiasm displayed and the value attached that all could have been used for the things and glory of God. Having these things are not wrong, but they may be distractions from God's activities.

Let's look at Luke 14:16-24.

> *Then said he unto him, A certain man made a great supper, and bade many: And sent his servant at supper time to say to them that were bidden, Come; for all things are now ready. And they all with one consent began to make excuse. The first said unto him, I have bought a piece of ground, and I must needs go and see it: I pray thee have me excused. And another said, I have bought five yoke of oxen, and I go to prove them: I pray thee have me excused. And another said, I have married a wife, and therefore I cannot come. So that servant came, and shewed his lord these things. Then the master of the house being angry said to his servant, Go out quickly into the streets and lanes of the city, and bring in hither the poor, and the maimed, and the halt, and the blind. And the servant said, Lord, it is done as thou hast commanded, and yet there is room. And the*

lord said unto the servant, Go out into the highways and hedges, and compel them to come in, that my house may be filled. For I say unto you, That none of those men which were bidden shall taste of my supper.

In this parable, invitations were extended to three men to attend a banquet prepared specifically for some guests. The servant went to tell them that the supper that was prepared for them was ready. Each of the three men that were invited had something else to do and made excuses. One had recently purchased a piece of land and needed to attend to it. Another had purchased five yoke of oxen and was ready to try them out. The third was recently married and simply said that he could not come. The master said that none of them would taste the food that was prepared. The bible says that he was angry. The master then gave the food to others. There was nothing wrong with having the land, the oxen or being married. Those are all legitimate things. The problem is that these things consumed their time and took priority over feasting with the master. God has prepared a feast of knowledge, ministry, wisdom, insight, discernment and Word for us has invited us to partake. We partake through our praise and worship services, Bible study, prayer meetings and ministry involvement. Many times we are so preoccupied with our things that we are in effect saying "no, thank you" to God for the feast prepared. Again, what a high spiritual price to pay for having the things. Let's begin to look at why we are making the purchases that we make.

Impulsive spending

Spending impulsively is when a purchase is made without thinking about it. No analysis or consideration is applied when making the purchase. The only driver of the decision is the emotions. It is a quick decision and not well thought out. Impulsive spending habits are difficult to identify because society endorses the "I deserve it" and "have it now" mentality. We constantly hear on the news about the debt that the average American has. When we hear this statistic, we begin to have these feelings/thoughts:

- I'm in this boat with a lot of people so it must be okay.
- It's expected that I would have debt
- It is normal to have credit card debt

Today we are bombarded with messages on television that entice us to indulge ourselves. The messages attempt to convince us that we deserve the best and that we can have the best. They also appeal to us by saying, "you can have it now". Buying into these messages leads to purchases that are outside of our means and not well thought out. Impulsive spending habits are developed because of lack of discipline and wisdom. The Bible speaks specifically about this temptation. In 1 John 2:15-16, John talks about divided loyalty. Keep in mind that he is speaking to Christians with varying levels of spiritual maturity. This is evident in 1 John 2:12-14 where he refers to fathers, young men and children. Therefore you are not excluded from the message here.

Verse 15: *Love not the world, neither the things that are in the world. If any man love the world, the love of the Father is not in him.*
John is commanding them not to continue to love the world itself or the things of the world now that they have received salvation. He is speaking of loyalty to the world in contrast to loyalty to God. If your loyalty is to the things of this world then, it cannot be to God. We can tell where your loyalty or love is by whether you are keeping God's commandments or not (John 14:15). The world is not inherently bad. The world and the things in it however, appeal to and have a close affiliation with our flesh. Our flesh is in opposition to the things of God. We find in Romans 8:7-8 where this is plainly stated—*Because the carnal mind is enmity against God: for it is not subject to the law of God, neither indeed can be. So then they that are in the flesh cannot please God.* When you love the world, you devote your ways, efforts and means toward it and the things in it. Therefore, you cannot also devote your ways, efforts and means toward the things of God.

Verse 16: *For all that is in the world, the lust of the flesh, and the lust of the eyes, and the pride of life, is not of the Father, but is of the world.*

Here he explains why we should cease that loving/loyal relationship to the world. John says that all that is in the world is not of the Father. He cites three powerful categories in which the things or temptations that are in the world fall within. The first category are those physical desires(lust of the flesh) that appeal to the body and promote indulgence of the flesh. The next category is personal desires (lust of the eyes). This category references the riches, possessions and other materialistic things that we are drawn to by our eyes. The last category refers to the selfish desires (pride of life). This includes those things that relate to social status, esteem and grandeur. The Amplified Bible refers to the pride of life as *"assurance in one's own resources or in the stability of earthly things"*. Read that again. Can you see how advertisers appeal to all of these in their messages to the public? The message is very subtle and appears harmless on the surface, but there is great hidden danger in entertaining them. Although the specific temptation may take on various forms and each of us may respond differently to the same temptation, they all fall within these three broad categories. It's what you see (eyes), what you feel you want (flesh) and what you feel you deserve or can have (pride). When we respond to these messages without applying wisdom and without thought, we are spending impulsively. Think back to the example of the digital camera. Based on the reasons for buying the camera, it can be considered an impulsive purchase. The purchase was simply the immediate reaction to a desire to have one. Making purchases of this type regularly can mean that you have developed impulsive spending habits. There may be several root causes to impulse spending. In order to identify it, you must be very honest with yourself and move beyond the surface of "I just wanted it".

Now that we know what it means to spend impulsively, let's discuss how you can break the cycle. The first step is to get the truth in your spirit about who owns the money that you are spending. Once you have done this, you must ensure that you are adhering to a detailed budget. Building a budget will be discussed later. Next, you must begin to develop the habit of praying about every purchase. I mean that literally!!! With every item that you desire to purchase, stop to pray before purchasing it. The desire to have certain things will not automatically go away because you have read this book. In fact, the impulse may get even stronger. **What you have to do is train your body and mind that your Spirit is in control. You must begin to demonstrate through prayer that you are submitting to the knowledge and wisdom of God about how to spend His money**. You do this by consulting Him about every purchase. I'm not asking you to stop, kneel and pray in the mall, but yield to the Holy Spirit by listening to and obeying Him wherever you are. I have experienced this on many levels. One of my habits was going to Wal-Mart and buying things just because they were "on sale". I stocked up on Rubbermaid items because I thought you could never have enough. I would just buy it because I liked the variety of colors and styles as well. I just had to have them. I would also do this with various other items in the store. Whether I really needed a particular item or not, I would put it in my basket because it was attractive or on sale. When I picked up something that I liked, but not necessarily needed, I remember saying quite often "I'm sure I can use this for something around the house". The Rubbermaid items and these other things were purchased with no purpose in mind. I looked for the reason after I got home. After I received the revelation about God's finances, I was determined to break that habit. I would still stock up the basket while in Wal-Mart, but I would end up purchasing only half of the items. While walking to the register, I would whisper a prayer. With each step I was convicted. By the time I got to the register, I would have put many items back. As I would put the remaining items on the belt, I would often tell the cashier "I've changed my mind about this item." My average trip to Wal-Mart went from $150 to $75!! Your item may not be found at Wal-Mart, but it could be in the mall, at the car dealership, on the internet or at the grocery store. Once you repent and pray, the Holy Spirit will nudge you when you are acting out of impulse rather than need. Now, I'm not saying that you should not buy some things that you want. The message here is to be wise about your choices and subject your fleshly desires to the Spirit in you.

Contentment—A Learned Behavior

Phil 4:10-13 *But I rejoiced in the Lord greatly, that now at the last your care of me hath flourished again; wherein ye were also careful, but ye lacked opportunity. [11]Not that I speak in respect of want: for I have learned, in whatsoever state I am, therewith to be content. [12] I know both how to be abased, and I know how to abound: every where and in all things I am instructed both to be full and to be hungry, both to abound and to suffer need. [13]I can do all things through Christ which strengtheneth me.*

One of the main reasons for uncontrolled spending is because we have not learned how to be content. For some reason, many people have equated contentment with "settling for less". We hear phrases like—"I'll just have to be content with this old couch for another year" or "I guess I will have to settle for this car for now". Being content is not settling for less. In fact, it couldn't be farther from the truth. The implication of settling is that you are not happy with the decision, but you don't have any other choice. If you settle for a particular type of car, then you are not happy with it, but you feel that you don't have another reasonable option. It also implies that you have lowered your standards. It is possible to settle for less without being content. **With contentment, there is an underlying joy and satisfaction with the situation or decision that was made.** In Philippians, Paul says that being content is a learned behavior (verse 11). Paul has learned how to be content through his actual life experiences. Paul had many hardships, one of which was being imprisoned. Through these life experiences, he learned to be satisfied in the current state that he found himself in at the time. That does not mean that he necessarily enjoyed the state that he was in or did not desire to get out of that state, but that he had learned to make the best of it. I believe that Paul probably found it relatively easy to find contentment because he had realistic expectations of his journey with the Lord. Paul was clear that suffering was going to be a part of his walk with God (Romans 8:17-18). Because of the clarity he had regarding his mission, he did not see contentment as a bad thing or his state as a permanent condition. He was focused on the eternal reward and recognized that these things were temporal.

Most importantly, Paul says that he learned to remain constant in his faith, his mission and his God regardless of the condition that he was in. He describes those conditions as being needy and having all needs met, as being hungry and being full. There are different emotions and temptations that exist in each of these conditions. Paul says, that he knew how to exist in any of these conditions and be satisfied. Paul had to be without at times to *learn* how much he could really live without. The key is verse 13—" *I can do all things through Christ that strengtheneth me.*" Paul attributes his ability to know how to be content to the divine grace of God. It was Christ who enabled him to maintain in those difficult and fruitful times. In order to learn contentment, it will take reliance on the grace of God and the strength of Jesus. It may also take us actually being in those various conditions to learn how to be content. If we fulfill every desire we have for things, the valuable lesson of contentment will not be learned. The world does not encourage contentment. We constantly hear that we can have a better car, bigger house, more gadgets, etc. Those things are nice and nothing is wrong with obtaining them. However, we must maintain the proper attitude and determine if it is necessary. There is a balance. The overall desire should be to seek God, and then you will not want for anything. In Psalm 34:10 we see that "the young lions do lack, and suffer hunger: but they that seek the LORD shall not want any good *thing.*"

Covetousness

Covetousness is a serious desire to own something (or someone) that belongs to another person. This is a significant factor in the spending habits of Christians today. Most do not believe that they covet because it is one of the Ten Commandments and we know we don't commit any of those sins, maybe others, but not those. Jesus warned of covetousness in Luke 12:15 when he said "Take heed, and beware of covetousness: for a man's life consisteth not in the abundance of the things which he possesseth. He then followed this with a parable that shows the destruction of the selfish. Gehazi, the servant of Elisha, is a good example of the downward spiral that can occur when you desire something that belongs to someone else. You can read the entire account in 2nd Kings 5:20-27. Elisha was instrumental in Naaman's healing of leprosy. Naaman offered Elisha compensation in return. Elisha did not accept the offer. Gehazi followed after Naaman to accept the offer on Elisha's behalf even though he was aware that Elisha did not accept the gifts. His intention was to accept the offer for himself. We have to beware of following after riches that do not belong to us. Before Gehazi even began to go after Naaman, he had a conversation with himself in verse 20. He made up his mind that he was going to get the gifts. He even made it sound spiritual when he said "as the Lord liveth". He said this as if it somehow made it the right thing to do. We do the same thing today. We will add the spiritual comment or reference to justify the covetous actions that we take. Doing this does not make it right. The first thing that Gehazi does is lie. When coveting, the first response is normally to lie. The lie is to make it seem like you are not being greedy or selfish. That is what Gehazi did. He was there when the initial offer was made and he witnessed Elisha's refusal. It would have looked bad to just say "I think that my master has made a mistake and I'll take it on his behalf. He lied and said that Elisha had reconsidered and sent him to accept the gift. It is sometimes difficult to explain to others why you bought the new car when you are in a tremendous amount of debt, have 2 other cars and are stressed out. Instead of saying the truth that there was an intense desire to have one because someone else does, the person will likely lie. The first lie led to another lie. When Elisha asked him where he had been he said nowhere. Elisha discerned the truth and corrected him. The end result is was that Gehazi was cursed with leprosy. Beware of seeking wealth, riches or things at all costs. It will lead to destruction.

Why is covetousness a sin? When you covet, your desire for the thing becomes more important than the will of God. You then in effect say that God is too slow in giving you what you need so you pursue the thing yourself. In following this intense desire, you disregard the will of God and begin to implement your own will. Once you get the thing that you wanted so badly, then you begin to cherish it and devote yourself totally to it. God is then no longer first in your life. In Colossians 3:5 Paul labeled this sin as idolatry—*"Mortify therefore your members which are upon the earth; fornication, uncleanness, inordinate affection, evil concupiscence, and covetousness, which is idolatry:*. It becomes spiritual idolatry because the respect and love that is due only to God has been transferred to worldly things. They begin to replace God.

CHAPTER 6
THE TRAP CALLED DEBT

One of the most subtle yet dangerous traps that the enemy has laid for us today is debt. Now of course, he does not call it debt, but the bottom line is the accumulation of significant amounts of debt. Let's get real clear about what debt truly is. You are in debt when you

- Obtain money that you did not earn (a line of credit, money from a friend, advance against a credit card)
- Owe money to someone for a purchase made on credit
- You are spending money that you don't have

We are made to believe today that it is okay to have some debt. It is not okay. Many times we are comfortable with debt as long as we are paying it off. While you are paying it off, you are still in debt if any amount is still owed. The media would have us to believe that we are a part of the norm if we have debt because the vast majority of Americans are in debt. It is not okay. More importantly, for Christians, it should not be the norm. Let's look at how being in debt relates to the principles we have already addressed:

- Interest is paid on debt. Paying this interest is not being a good steward of God's money. There is no return being gained on these funds.
- You cannot serve two masters. The creditor dictates to you what is owed, when and what interest rate you will repay. The creditor becomes your master.

The Bible has a lot to say about debt. I will take the time to address many of the scripture references on debt in great detail in order to provide you with the truth to replace the lies the enemy has planted regarding personal debt.

Romans 13:8—*Owe no man anything, but to love one another, for he that loveth another hath fulfilled the law.* The context of chapter 13 is to give what is owed to those that rule over you. We are not to hold back honor, custom or support to whom it is due. Thus, in verse 8, we are not to owe it, but give those things when it is due. When we are in debt, the creditor in this case is ruler over us. The message here is that if you have it, get from under it expediently. I believe that all knowing God anticipated that we may have occasion to obtain credit. His expectation is that we do not stay in debt, but that we pay it off when it is due.

Proverbs 22:7—*The rich ruleth over the poor, and the borrower is servant to the lender.* Here wisdom tells us that a person that borrows becomes a servant to the creditor. A servant is one who is under the master's control and bound by whatever parameters the master has designed. A servant does not have the same level of freedom that others have. So, when you borrow, you become a slave to the creditor. Practically, this is very true. When you owe someone, you are bound by the parameters of the repayment schedule, interest rate and other terms and conditions of the agreement. Although you may be able to negotiate the rate, it is still at the discretion of the creditor. In order to meet the terms and conditions of repayment, almost every facet of your life is controlled by the obligation to repay. You are a servant to the creditor. Your level of freedom becomes impacted because you may not be able to purchase certain items or give to certain causes because of the current obligations to repay. So, you see, the debt causes you to become a slave!!! Think about the things that you cannot do because you are in debt.

Deuteronomy 28:44-47—*He shall lend to thee, and thou shalt not lend to him: he shall be the head, and thou shalt be the tail. Moreover all these curses shall come upon thee, and shall pursue thee, and overtake thee, till thou be destroyed; because thou hearkenedst not unto the voice of the LORD thy God, to keep his* commandments and his statutes which he commanded thee be upon thee for a sign and for a wonder, and upon thy seed for ever. Because thou servedst not the LORD thy God with joyfulness, and with gladness of heart, for the abundance of all things. It is considered a curse in the Old Testament to borrow from someone. To borrow not only brought the curse upon the individual, but also their children.

Psalm 37:21—*The wicked borroweth, and payeth not again: but the righteous sheweth mercy, and giveth.* A person that borrows and does not repay is considered wicked. This is a famous chapter of Psalm that is often referred to when we want to encourage someone not to worry about people that are mistreating them. We are quick to tell them "fret not thyself because of evildoers". Well, included in this same chapter is reference to those that do not repay their debts. They are considered in the same category as the "evildoers".

Proverbs 3:27-28—*Withhold not good from them to whom it is due, when it is in the power of thine hand to do it. Say not unto thy neighbour, Go, and come again, and tomorrow I will give; when thou hast it by thee.* This one may be a tough one to digest for some of us. In its simplest terms the scripture is telling us to repay what is owed. We should not make decisions to spend money on a non-essential item when that money should be used to reduce debt. For example, all other things being equal, Janice has an extra $100 this month due to retirement of one of her debt. She owes a creditor $1,400 and she has already made the minimum payment for this month. She decides that she is going to buy that designer purse she has always wanted. It fulfills a desire and it would sure look nice with an outfit she has. Wisdom of this proverb tells us that it is better to pay that money to someone that she owes. She has the ability to expedite paying off this debt and should take the opportunity to do so. Do you agree? What would you do with the extra $100?

Inherent Assumptions About Debt

There are some key assumptions that we make when we get into debt. We don't think about these on a daily basis because we are blinded to the truth when it comes to debt. This truth is often watered down or totally overshadowed by the marketing and media messages we see on a daily basis. Randy Alcorn, author of *Money, Possessions and Eternity*, lists six key assumptions involved in what he calls the "debt mentality":

1. We need more than God has given us.
2. God doesn't know best what our needs are.
3. God has failed to provide for our needs, forcing us to take matters into our own hands.
4. If God doesn't come through the way we think He should, we can find another way. Abraham tried this approach, which proved dishonoring to God (Genesis 16:2)
5. Just because today's income is sufficient to make our debt payments, tomorrow's will be too.
6. Our circumstances won't change—our health will be good, we'll keep our present job, our salary will keep up with inflation, and God won't direct us to another job with a lower salary or lead us to increase our giving.

When we incur debt, we make an assumption that we will be around to repay or that funds will be available to repay in the future. We assume that the current job salary will continue, no additional expenses will arise that will require the funds and that we will have the means to pay. I know that we don't normally think of these when incurring debt, but it is actually what are actions are saying. We are warned against this presumption in James 4:13-15: *Go to now, ye that say, To day or to morrow we will go into such a city, and continue there a year, and buy and sell, and get gain: Whereas ye know not what shall be on the morrow. For what is your life? It is even a vapour, that appeareth for a little time, and then vanisheth away. For that ye ought to say, If the Lord will, we shall live, and do this, or that.* The pridefulness of taking each day as if we have earned it is cautioned against in this scripture. God must be considered in all that we do. He must remain as the final authority of all of life's activities. A good example of this is when we charge something that is interest free for a certain amount of time (i.e., 90 days or 12 months). The mentality we have with these types of charges is that we will pay it off within the allotted time so it is really not debt. We feel that we are not wasting money in this case since interest will not be paid. Well, it is actually still a debt. You have received goods for which you have not paid yet. You are still expected to pay for it. At some point in the future, you are assuming you will have the funds to pay it off before interest begins to accrue. We must avoid this lure of advertising. We see "interest free" and automatically think "free". Well, it is not free; you must still pay for it. Business owners are very aware of the national trends on consumer debt, the current unemployment rate and the likelihood that most people will not pay it off by the date before which interest begins to accrue. All of these factors are favorable for the business, not the consumer. The traps here is that if you do not pay it off within that "interest free" period, interest will accrue and be owed from the *date of purchase*. When we go into debt for an item, we may be saying that God has not supplied the resources to meet all of our needs. We also need to be careful with associating debt-related decisions with God's will. God does not contradict Himself, His will is made clear in His Word. Many times we will say that we are going to apply for the line of credit, loan or charge card and if it is approved then it must be God's will that we obtain the credit to do whatever it is that we want or need. God has said over and over again in His Word how he feels about debt and the unfavorable and burdensome position that it puts us in. Why would it be His will to put us in that position? Remember, that going into debt is a decision. Before going into debt, you should consider the practical and spiritual consequences.

The Elaborate Plot—Putting It All Together

By now you should see how the enemy has crafted an elaborate plot to keep the people of God in bondage to their finances and away from the prosperity that God has promised us. All of it hinges on one very important scripture that is found in Hosea 4:6 *My people are destroyed for lack of knowledge: because thou has rejected knowledge, I will reject thee, that thou shalt be no priest to me: seeing thous hast forgotten the law of they God, I will also forget thy children.* The context of this particular scripture is that the people were in opposition to the priest. It was the priest's job to share the wisdom and knowledge of God with the people to give them direction. In this case, the people did not want to hear it; therefore they lacked the knowledge to perform according to God's will. They were receiving the information, they chose to reject it. So begins the plot.

It takes money to live.

Money is required to have the things I want in life.

I have to work to make money to get the things I want in life.

I have to work 2 or 3 jobs to get the things that money can buy.

I have to work a lot of overtime to pay my bills.

I tithe.

I have a certain lifestyle that I desire or must maintain; I cannot lose any of my current income.

I work everyday, so I deserve to have what I want.

I can charge things every once in a while since I do have a steady source of income.

With both of us working, surely we can have nice cars to drive.

It's my money to do with it as I please.

At least I'm not blowing the money on frivolous things.

I can't participate in the ministry of my calling because of the hours that I have to work.

I gave God His 10%.

These bills are mounting.

I live to work and I work to live.

I can't take a vacation this year.

I cant' seem to get out of this hole.

I have a bad attitude every day now.

I hate this job. (the same job that bought the things I wanted earlier)

I need another job.

I'm going to have to declare bankruptcy.

Destruction, despair, desperation, doubt about the future, devastation.

Departure from your Divine Destiny.

The framework supporting all of this is that there is no biblical teaching in the local church on how to avoid getting trapped in this plot or more importantly how to be delivered from this. It is more serious than telling your spiritual friends that you need a financial blessing. Without sound teaching by the local church on God's view of finances, the plot thickens because there exists then a lack of knowledge on the part of the people. The people referenced in Hosea 4:6 were destroyed because they <u>rejected</u> the knowledge. There was a means or way prepared to obtain the required information and knowledge, but it was rejected. When Pastors do not provide the knowledge according to God's word then they are rejecting it as well. Woe unto them!! If the word is given and the people reject it, woe unto them. God has given us His powerful word concerning money and finances, yet we reject it, thus bringing about our own destruction. We either say or hear the following—

"Pastor only needs to worry about the 10% I give to him, I can handle the rest."

"The Lord would want me to have these nice things since I represent Him."

"God only expects tithes and offerings."

In each of these statements, knowledge is rejected from the Pastor. We don't go to great lengths to seek the knowledge of the Word regarding our finances. The consequence for their rejection of the knowledge of God is that He rejected them and stripped them of their royalty. He removed the priestly privileges from the people. The honor and benefits were taken away. What a price to pay for rejecting the knowledge of God. Today, many of us are in the financial situation we are in because we have rejected the knowledge of God. So you see the plot is to keep us ignorant about what God has to say about money so that we can remain in a destructive state, living beneath our means and absent of the honor that was originally placed with us.

CHAPTER 7
THE HEART OF THE MATTER

In reviewing what you have read so far, it should be very apparent that the core of our spending and other personal financial situations is a matter of the heart. Jesus plainly addresses this in a powerful message in Matthew 6:19-24.

> *Lay not up for yourselves treasures upon earth, where moth and rust doth corrupt, and where thieves break through and steal: But lay up for yourselves treasures in heaven, where neither moth nore rust doth corrupt, and where thieves do not break through nor steal: For where your treasure is, there will your heart be also. But if thine eye be evil, thy whole body shall be full of darkness. If therefore the light that is in thee be darkness, how great is that darkness! No man can serve two masters: for either he will hate the one, and love the other; or else he will hold to the one, and despise the other. Ye cannot serve God and mammon.*

The topic here is where the treasure is laid up. A treasure is something that has value and sentiment attached to it. It is personalized value. I may treasure my high school class ring because of the struggle to attain the diploma. You may not treasure yours as much. Because of the value and emotions that I attach to my ring, I put forth extra effort and energy to make sure that is always clean, kept in a safe place and always in good shape. You may keep yours in a jewelry box and only clean it when you plan to wear it to the class reunion. The same ring, just different value attached to it. Whatever you treasure, you have your heart set on it. So you see, Jesus was addressing the heart here, not the money itself. He instructs us to lay our treasures in heaven because it is eternal instead of on earth where it is temporal. He's saying that our efforts, energy and attention should be directed toward those things that yield eternal benefits, not temporal benefits. Another way of saying this is that we are not to attach so much "treasure-like" value to temporal things. He tells us that these temporal or earthly things are subject to moths (clothes), rust (machinery, silver, gold) and thieves (anything they think is valuable). We are to attach value to the things of God because they are not subject to moths, rust or thieves. The reason this is important is because **wherever your treasure is, there will your heart be—your energy, your priorities, your demands, your strength, your mind, your desires.** I love this definition of mammon given in Matthew Henry's Commentary on the Bible (1997)

> *Mammon* is a Syriac word, that signifies gain; so that whatever in this world is, or is accounted by us to be, *gain* (Phil. 3:7), is *mammon. Whatever is in the world, the lust of the flesh, the lust of the eye, and the pride of life,* is *mammon.* To some their belly is their *mammon,* and they serve that (Phil. 3:19); to others their ease, their sleep, their sports and pastimes, are their *mammon* (Prov. 6:9); to others worldly riches (James 4:13); to others honours and preferments; the praise and applause of men was the Pharisees' *mammon;* in a word, self, the unity in which the world's trinity centres, sensual, secular self, is the *mammon* which cannot be served in conjunction with *God;* for if it be served, it is in competition with him and in contradiction to him.

Notice that Jesus did not say that you *should not* do this, he said that you *can not.* This implies that there will come a point when a choice must be made about which side you will choose. There is no straggling the fence on this one. Wherever your heart truly is, that is what you will be drawn to. In summary, when you are constantly focused on and seeking riches or more money for the sake of "storing it up", that is truly where your heart is. You can tithe and still be storing up things on earth.

Anxiety is directly related to what is in our heart concerning material things. Let's look at Matthew 6:31-33 *Therefore take no thought, saying, What shall we eat? or, What shall we drink? or, Wherewithal shall we be clothed?* *32(For after all these things do the Gentiles seek:) for your heavenly Father knoweth that ye have need of all these things.* *33But seek ye first the kingdom of God, and his righteousness; and all these things shall be added unto you.* Inserted parenthetically is an often overlooked, yet key sentence in verse 32. Jesus says that seeking after these things is a practice of the Gentiles or the heathens. At this time, the Gentiles worshipped idols yet they did not look to these gods to supply them with their needs therefore they are filled with the cares of the world. They did not have anyone to look to in order to address the concerns of this world so they carried those burdens themselves. For Christians, though, we have a Heavenly Father who knows that we have need of these things. There is a distinction drawn here that is very important. He's showing a contrast here between the Christians and the Gentiles. You cannot claim or profess to be a Christian yet are bound by worry due to the cares of this world. Verse 33 begins with the word BUT. It begins as an alternative to what is mentioned previously—worrying about these material things. It means instead of spending mental energy and time that leads to anxiety, here's something else to occupy that time with. SEEK YE FIRST. The Greek word for seek here, ZETEO, means to strive after, to desire, to aim at. It is in the present tense. It means a continual or constant striving after. I like how David described his longing or seeking after God while in the wilderness in Psalm 63. David says:

God, thou art my God; early will I seek thee: my soul thirsteth for thee, my flesh longeth for thee in a dry and thirsty land, where no water is; 2To see thy power and thy glory, so as I have seen thee in the sanctuary.

71

David says I will seek you early because I do not want to miss you. It is a priority for him, it is how he will start his day. Then he says in verse 8—*My soul followeth hard after thee: thy right hand upholdeth me.* His whole being is engaged in the pursuit of God. Again David's desire is to hold on to and continue in communion with God. When you make seeking God a priority, you significantly limit the level of anxiety about the cares of this world. Your time, energy, efforts, finances are all geared toward heavenly goals.

Let's be practical about this now. Think about when you wanted that college degree, when you wanted that job, that house, that position, or whatever you really wanted in life. How did you prepare for it, what did you sacrifice for it, what did you give up for it and why? You were earnestly seeking after the end result with your whole heart. Even if the completion of your education took a little longer than anticipated, did you give up? What if someone else got the job? Did you just quit? If these things were important enough to you, then the answer is NO because it was a priority and you were seeking and pursuing those things. Here Jesus is saying seek first the kingdom of God. He says **let the cares of the kingdom supersede the cares of this world.** There is nothing wrong with desiring material things, which is fine, as long as that desire is not placed above your desire for the things of God. When faced with choices, we must choose the things of God first. Sometimes we have to rearrange our priorities and ensure that we are seeking the things of God. It means sacrifice sometimes.

What is the kingdom of God? It is the sovereign rule, dominion of God. It is the realm in which God has authority over every aspect of your life. Jesus is saying seek to have God rule your heart, your mind, your actions, your will, YOU. Please understand that the kingdom of God is not a place and it has no geographical boundaries. I believe this is where we often get confused. We often quote this scripture without a full understanding of the Kingdom of God. In many hearts and minds when this scripture is read or preached, is a thought of seeking God by going to church or paying tithes. Yes that it part of it, but the kingdom of God is so much more than that. It is where God RULES and REIGNS. Going to church and seeking His will is great, but if He is not ruler of our hearts, then we're not there yet. Jesus says we are to pursue and strive to have God as Supreme Ruler of our life. That requires everyone else, including yourself, to get off of the throne of your life. He also instructs us to seek the characteristics of the kingdom. It reads, Seek ye first the kingdom of God **and** His righteousness. Righteousness is the sum total of all the requirements of God. He's saying that we must seek the character and the quality of being just. Jesus is saying that it must be a priority to have God rule our lives and that we must seek the characteristics of being just. Remember that character is something that is expressed. It will become obvious in your interactions with others if you have His character or not. You can look at your spending habits, your lifestyle and actions to determine if God is first or not. We would never admit that He is not since it would cause you to be a hypocrite, but your actions will tell it all.

❑ **Complete The Heart Of The Matter worksheet.**

CHAPTER 8
BIBLICAL PROSPERITY

There are many sermons preached today about prosperity. In fact, the prosperity message is included in almost every sermon about faith. Years ago, the very opposite message was being preached. I heard many times that God was a friend to the poor. I heard that the more money you had, the more wicked you were. I even believed that Jesus was poor and since He is our Elder Brother, then we too must be poor to be "like Him". You were considered to be really spiritual if you were poor. I believed that the riches of the world served to distract you from having fellowship with God. I remember Mark 8:34 being used as the hinge for these beliefs. The scripture reads *And when he had called the people unto him with his disciples also, he said unto them, Whosoever will come after me, let him deny himself, and take up his cross, and follow me.* The emphasis was placed on denying yourself of worldly things in order to follow Jesus. Then I began hearing the exact opposite. The messages that I have heard primarily focus on how God wants us to be prosperous. The message is now is that you are really spiritual if you are living in prosperity. Before I learned how to study the Word of God for myself and gained divine insight, I believed

- This was suddenly the time that God was finally going to release His abundance for us.
- If you are not walking or living in prosperity, then you are doing something wrong.
- The definition of prosperity was limited to money.
- All it takes is faith in what God says about prosperity to begin to have it.

While it is true that the Bible has a lot to say about prosperity and wealth, the scriptures are often taken out of context in order to appeal to a materialistic society. Most Christians find themselves at one extreme or the other—poverty or materialism. Earlier we discussed the fact that money has no inherent value and is morally neutral, keep that in mind. In the next section we will look at prosperity in the Old Testament and in the New Testament.

Prosperity in the Old Testament

Obedience. There are many examples in the Old Testament where God's reward for obedience was abundance or prosperity. Poverty was always the consequence of not obeying God. Deuteronomy 28:1-13 is often quoted when referring to the material things that God will provide.

> *And it shall come to pass, if thou shalt hearken diligently unto the voice of the LORD thy God, to observe and to do all his commandments which I command thee this day, that the LORD thy God will set thee on high above all nations of the earth: ²And all these blessings shall come on thee, and overtake thee, if thou shalt hearken unto the voice of the LORD thy God. ³Blessed shalt thou be in the city, and blessed shalt thou be in the field. ⁴Blessed shall be the fruit of thy body, and the fruit of thy ground, and the fruit of thy cattle, the increase of thy kine, and the flocks of thy sheep. ⁵Blessed shall be thy basket and thy store. ⁶Blessed shalt thou be when thou comest in, and blessed shalt thou be when thou goest out. ⁷The LORD shall cause thine enemies that rise up against thee to be smitten before thy face: they shall come out against thee one way, and flee before thee seven ways. ⁸The LORD shall command the blessing upon thee in thy storehouses, and in all that thou settest thine hand unto; and he shall bless thee in the land which the*

LORD thy God giveth thee. [9]The LORD shall establish thee an holy people unto himself, as he hath sworn unto thee, if thou shalt keep the commandments of the LORD thy God, and walk in his ways. [10]And all people of the earth shall see that thou art called by the name of the LORD; and they shall be afraid of thee. [11]And the LORD shall make thee plenteous in goods, in the fruit of thy body, and in the fruit of thy cattle, and in the fruit of thy ground, in the land which the LORD sware unto thy fathers to give thee. [12]The LORD shall open unto thee his good treasure, the heaven to give the rain unto thy land in his season, and to bless all the work of thine hand: and thou shalt lend unto many nations, and thou shalt not borrow. [13]And the LORD shall make thee the head, and not the tail; and thou shalt be above only, and thou shalt not be beneath; if that thou hearken unto the commandments of the LORD thy God, which I command thee this day, to observe and to do them:,

We often focus on the blessings only, but the blessings were contingent upon their obedience to the commandments of God. The blessings would be released when they "*hearken diligently unto the voice of the LORD thy God, to observe and to <u>do all his commandments</u>*". It is rare to hear anyone even make reference to the consequences for not obeying God. They can be found in the very next 54 verses in the same chapter. There are numerous curses mentioned for disobedience. We must ensure that we are getting the complete story when discussing the blessings of God. Yes, it is true that God desires to bless His people, but it is equally true that He expects obedience first. It is incorrect to believe that you can give generously to the kingdom of God and expect for Him to make you prosperous without obedience. Obedience to His commandments is required. Giving is not a command, but rather an expectation.

Warnings. There are also warnings of the dangers of prosperity found in the Old Testament.

> Deuteronomy 8:10-18 *When thou hast eaten and art full, then thou shalt bless the LORD thy God for the good land which he hath given thee. [11]Beware that thou forget not the LORD thy God, in not keeping his commandments, and his judgments, and his statutes, which I command thee this day: [12]Lest when thou hast eaten and art full, and hast built goodly houses, and dwelt therein; [13]And when thy herds and thy flocks multiply, and thy silver and thy gold is multiplied, and all that thou hast is multiplied; [14]Then thine heart be lifted up, and thou forget the LORD thy God, which brought thee forth out of the land of Egypt, from the house of bondage; [15]Who led thee through that great and terrible wilderness, wherein were fiery serpents, and scorpions, and drought, where there was no water; who brought thee forth water out of the rock of flint; [16]Who fed thee in the wilderness with manna, which thy fathers knew not, that he might humble thee, and that he might prove thee, to do thee good at thy latter end; [17]And thou say in thine heart, My power and the might of mine hand hath gotten me this wealth. [18]But thou shalt remember the LORD thy God: for it is he that giveth thee power to get wealth, that he may establish his covenant which he sware unto thy fathers, as it is this day.*

This scripture is really self-explanatory. It outlines the things that the Israelites should remember when they experience increase. They are encouraged not to forget God and what He had done for them in the past. We are to always recall what God has already done for us. One purpose for this is that it prompts us to remember God in the time of plenty. It is important to remember how He provided and met the needs so that we can be reminded that He is a Provider. Doing this puts us in a mode of thanksgiving and prompts us to recall the character of God. When we focus on who He is, we no longer focus on what we have. We just know that He is good, faithful, kind, mighty, patient and a deliverer among many more wonderful characteristics. They are told to remember that it is God that gave them the power to get the things. This keeps them from transferring their devotion from Him to the possessions. He tells them to remember that the **prosperity has a purpose**. The purpose was to fulfill the agreement or covenant that He made with their forefathers. Whenever we prosper, there is a divine purpose attached to it. We have to be careful not to attribute the prosperity to our intellect or ability and seek to understand the divine purpose we are to fulfill with it.

Giving. The book of Proverbs contains many references to wealth. In fact it is one of the major themes of the book. The cornerstone on the wisdom regarding wealth is found in Proverbs 3:9-10—*Honour the LORD with thy substance, and with the first-fruits of all thine increase: So shall thy barns be filled with plenty, and thy presses shall burst out with new wine.* Having plenty comes when God is honored first. You have to be active in the cycle of giving that was explained in Chapter 4 to be prosperous. To honor the Lord is to give to Him what is required and what is requested. When this is done, the prosperity comes forth. Notice that the barns and presses will prosper. There must be a greater harvest to fill the barns and the presses. With the greater harvest, or increase, there is more to give and to honor God with.

Why do the wicked prosper? This question was raised several times throughout the Old Testament. David in Psalm 37:35 and 73:3,12 inquired as to why the wicked increase in wealth. Jeremiah, who was a righteous man also boldly asked God in Jeremiah 12:1 *Righteous art thou, O LORD, when I plead with thee: yet let me talk with thee of thy judgments: Wherefore doth the way of the wicked prosper? wherefore are all they happy that deal very treacherously?* The fact that they raised the question indicates the perceived association between wealth and God's approval by the Old Testament believers. They believed that it was not a just thing for God to bestow wealth upon the wicked. We need only look at the life of Joseph to see that this is not the case. He was faithful to God yet he experienced both times of prosperity and adversity. Job is another classic example that God does not show His disapproval by allowing poverty. Job's accusers/comforters assumed that there must have been some hidden sin in his life that led to his loss of wealth. The Bible says that God approved of Job, yet He allowed him to experience extreme adversity. The examples of Job and Joseph demonstrate that **God's sovereignty is a key component in gaining prosperity.** God chooses whom He will bless. It is His right to shower down blessings on whomever He pleases and to withhold them as well. It is His choice as to how much He will entrust to each individual. This question should not preoccupy us. God has His reasons for everything that He does. After much thought on this topic, David began to realize that the end of the prospering wicked is eternal punishment. We see this in Psalm 73:16-19. In the Amplified Bible, it reads

> *But when I considered how to understand this, it was too great an effort for me and too painful. Until I went into the sanctuary of God; then I understood [for I considered] their end. [After all] you do set the [wicked] in slippery places; you cast them down to ruin and destruction. How they become a desolation in a moment! They are utterly consumed with terrors!*

David indicates that the very thought of why he saw the wicked prospering was painful and took up a lot of his energy and effort. He says in verses 21-22 that his *"heart was grieved, ebittered, and in a state of ferment, and I was pricked in my heart...So foolish, stupid and brutish was I, and ignorant; I was like a beast before You"*. Wow, look at how the very thought that others were prospering changed David's whole personality and character. Why is this? Like us, David focused on what he saw externally instead of what was really going on internally. We are always trying to figure out how certain people have attained what they have. We also want to be in a position to determine who should have what and how much. This takes away precious time from improving our own personal matters. David took this question to God and God showed him some things. He opened up David's eyes to see what was really going on. David settled the whole matter by saying in verse 28 *"But it is good for me to draw near to god; I have put my trust in the Lord God and made Him my refuge, that I may tell of all Your works."* He returned the focus to his own personal relationship with God. His relationship with God then began to consume his time, thoughts and efforts. We would do well to follow David's example and re-focus our thoughts on the things of God.

Prosperity and The New Testament

It is very obvious in the gospels that the Pharisees retained the mentality of the Old Testament—that God's disapproval resulted in a curse upon you. At one point even the disciples displayed this attitude when they came upon the blind man. They asked Jesus in John 9:2 Master, who did sin, this man, or his parents, that he was born blind? Jesus responded by saying *that Neither hath this man sinned, nor his parents: but that the works of God should be made manifest in him.* Jesus was saying that God had a higher purpose in mind when He allowed the blindness in the man. Again, God is sovereign and cannot be bound by our rules and expectations. Jesus said in Matthew 5:45 *That ye may be the children of your Father which is in heaven: for he maketh his sun to rise on the evil and on the good, and sendeth rain on the just and on the unjust.* He was speaking in the context of loving everyone. He's saying that since God allows the blessings of sun and rain on both the just and the unjust, we can't discriminate on who we love by what we see on the outside. Related to wealth though, this scripture shows us that God, in His sovereignty, can shower blessings on whomever He chooses, whether they are just or unjust.

When it comes to prosperity messages, keep in mind that God's view of prosperity is different from the world's view. The world views prosperity as the attainment of wealth and riches. God has a spiritual system that He uses to evaluate and measure prosperity.

Revelation 3:17 shows us that it is possible to have riches and yet be poor spiritually *Because thou sayest, I am rich, and increased with goods, and have need of nothing; and knowest not that thou art wretched, and miserable, and poor, and blind, and naked*: The sad commentary here is that the people did not even realize or know that they were poor, blind and naked. The riches gave them a false sense of spiritual security. This highlights the danger of preaching an incomplete message on prosperity. Obedience, giving, and most importantly God's sovereignty must be expounded upon for the people to fully understand biblical prosperity. My mother is a great example of someone that is financially poor, but I believe is extremely prosperous. She is a woman of faith and conviction that loves the Lord. She is rich towards God. More importantly she has peace and joy that goes beyond the joy and peace I have seen in wealthy people.

Finally, when the prosperity message is preached and studied, we need to be instructed on how to live with the riches when it come to us. The warnings of spiritual danger outlined in 1st Timothy 6:17-19 should be taught—*Charge them that are rich in this world, that they be not highminded, nor trust in uncertain riches, but in the living God, who giveth us richly all things to enjoy; That they do good, that they be rich in good works, ready to distribute, willing to communicate; Laying up in store for themselves a good foundation against the time to come, that they may lay hold on eternal life.* The rich are warned against becoming conceited and having confidence in the things instead of God. The rich are also instructed to give as well.

The Proper Perspective on 3 John 2

Beloved, I wish above all things that thou mayest prosper and be in health, even as thy soul prospereth.

The word prosper is the Greek word eudoo. This prosperity occurs with the soul as well as with respect to physical well-being, means literally to "have a pleasant trip," and denotes "getting along well." Very often this scripture is quoted as "God says that He wishes that we prosper..." It is clear from reading the first two verses that this is John's prayer for his friend Gaius. The term prosper is taken out of context and put into our english definition.

The bottom line on prosperity can be found in 1st Chronicles 29:11-12 *Thine, O LORD, is the greatness, and the power, and the glory, and the victory, and the majesty: for all that is in the heaven and in the earth is thine; thine is the kingdom, O LORD, and thou art exalted as head above all. ¹²Both riches and honour come of thee, and thou reignest over all; and in thine hand is power and might; and in thine hand it is to make great, and to give strength unto all.* If we spend time teaching the truth of this scripture then we would realize that God is truly in control of everything. Every obedient Christian will not live in prosperity as the world defines it, but will prosper spiritually. It is totally up to God to distribute His riches the way that He desires. Now, having said that, I firmly believe that it is God's desire that we experience financial prosperity, but you must fully understand spiritual prosperity first. The objective of this chapter was to place prosperity in its proper perspective and context. There are many scriptures that illustrate the point that we should expect to prosper and experience the wealthy places in God. These scriptures are not explored in this book. After you have matured in the various areas outlined in the book, I strongly encourage you to move away from the elementary teachings and pursue additional reading on prosperity.

Before you begin the next section of the book, please make sure that you have completed each worksheet. These worksheets will assist you in building an effective and realistic budget.

CHAPTER 9
BUDGETING

In this chapter we will review the basics of budgeting. Keep in mind that the focus of this book is to prepare your heart and mind to agree with God's plan for your finances. This chapter emphasizes the matters of the heart related to developing a budget. There are great resources available to provide very detailed steps to build a budget. I strongly recommend that you consult those resources to construct your final budget.

> *Prov. 27:23—24 Be thou diligent to know the state of thy flocks, and look well to thy herds. 24For riches are not for ever: and doth the crown endure to every generation?*

Now that you realize that the money and things belong to God and you feel a greater sense of responsibility to Him, how do you make sure you are making wise decisions? If you have truly transferred the ownership back where it belongs, you should feel a sense of freedom and healthy anxiety. The anxiety should be due to the increased sense of accountability for God's things.

- Where is the money going?
- I thought I would have $50 extra this week?
- I wish I could afford to _____?
- If I didn't have to buy new tires for the car, then I would be able to buy that _____I wanted.
- What do I have to show for the money?
- I would sure like to bless the Pastor this week with a monetary gift.
- How am I going to pay for a new watch?

Have you asked yourself any of these questions or similar ones lately? We have all asked them at one time or another. If you are going to be held accountable for your expenditures, you need a tool to track and plan for them. Planning for expected and unexpected expenditures is the sole reason for budgeting. Without a budget, how will you know where your money is going? Without a budget, your money is controlling you instead of you controlling it. A budget is a roadmap to your spending. It guides your finances in the direction that you send it per the budget. Most people fail to budget because they have the perception that a budget is too confining and restrictive. The real reason is that there is no sense of accountability for the spending. Let's pretend that you are planning to take a trip to New Mexico for your sister's wedding and you have never been there before. You plan to drive your car the entire trip. One of the first things that you will do is obtain directions from a map. You will determine your exact location for departure and your destination. You will then plan out the following:

- how long it should take, based on the miles, route you plan to take and your planned arrival date
- determine which landmarks you will pass in case you want to do some sightseeing
- consider the weather and terrain you must travel
- how much money you will need for gas, food, lodging and incidentals

Once you have these items identified, you will then plan for a successful trip. You will feel confident knowing where you are going because you have taken the time to plan the details of the trip. You will know the appropriate exits to take, the recommended hotels for lodging and significant landmarks to look for. With your roadmap for the trip, you will not be thrown off by unexpected weather conditions or other detours. Now suppose you did not plan the details of this trip and decided to leave on Saturday to arrive to the wedding in New Mexico on Wednesday. You figured you would just follow the signs and you can't go wrong. If the weather conditions become unfavorable and cause you to detour for a period of time, you are likely to be thrown off of your schedule. In addition, you will have to search for decent lodging because you didn't plan ahead. You may also end up late for the wedding. Even if you make it on time, you may be stressed, broke and tired.

Budgeting is your financial road map. If you plan to retire at a certain age, buy a home, get out of debt, pay for college, take a vacation, etc. then you need a road map on how to get there. Just like planning the trip to New Mexico, budgeting requires planning to ensure that you have a stress free, well financed trip. When the master returns for you to give an account of where the money is and how it has been used, you have to give an answer. A budget is the tool to assist you in giving this answer. Think of it even on a monthly basis. God has entrusted you with a month's worth of salary. He expects that you will use His finances that He enabled you to earn to meet your needs and any other instructions that He gives regarding how to use the money. The end of the month comes and you haven't done what He asked and He inquires as to what happened. How do you think "I don't know where it went" will go over with Him? Do you think He will entrust you with more the next time? A budget will at least provide the framework for a response.

The Lie About Budgeting

There is a common myth and trap of the enemy that says if you are paying your bills on time, making ends meet and you have a little extra money in your pocket then you don't need to budget. This is not true. If you believe this then you will not look beyond the surface of your present condition and accept what you see. Looking beyond the surface is what leads to the abundant life. If you are just paying your bills on time, then you don't necessarily review the details of your bills or the reason that you have the bill. For example, if you are paying your wireless bill and long distance bill on time each month, then you will probably never consider eliminating your long distance bill at home. You could eliminate your home long distance bill and utilize your wireless phone during off peak hours to make long distance calls. You would never consider that without seeing your financial picture and goals written down. The trap is complacency and as long as I'm not in a bind, then there is no need to change things. You don't feel a struggle to pay the bills, so you don't see a need to budget. Another popular misunderstanding is that a budget is too restrictive. The very nature of a budget is flexible. It is only a tool to provide guidelines for spending. It can be adjusted or amended as needed. The reason some believe that it restricts them too much is because of the discipline it demands to stick with the budget. When a budget is developed the lifestyle that you desire to lead is built into it. If restrictions exist in a budget, then it is intentionally included to assist in achieving the desired financial goals that have been established.

The Word—The Truth About Budgeting

In Proverb 27:23 we are called to be diligent to know the state of our business and to inspect it. Although the scripture makes reference to cattle and herds, it is applicable to our financial affairs. The flocks are the rancher's source of wealth, his basic assets. In order to ensure that the cattle produce the income he needs, he must pay close attention to their well being and care for them. We are to pay attention to our assets and other sources of wealth. To know in this scripture means to understand. To look well is to pay careful attention to. We are instructed to be diligent to understand and pay attention to our finances. We are to pay attention to ensure that it is well taken care of and to make sure that opportunities are not passing us by. The learning point in this scripture is also that effort must be put forth to understand our financial picture. It takes time, counsel, research and effort to understand the condition, outlook and well being of your assets and other financial matters. Flocks can get away easier than the herd can. You have to understand what it takes to keep them at home. The flock can be those small things that can get away from you in your budget (i.e., eating out, tolls, cards, etc.). We are also instructed to pay careful attention the larger financial items(the herds) that can provide the greatest return. Herds are larger than flock and the loss of one can pose a great financial burden. Pay close attention to those things that can break your financial back. Without a budget, you will not even know what those things are. They will come upon you before you know it if you are not paying attention.

Preparing and living by a budget requires diligence and effort. It is the tool to assist you in assessing the "state of your flocks". Let's put it all together now—

- The money and possessions belong to God
- He has placed us as stewards of His money
- He expects us to manage the money wisely
- He will hold us accountable for how we spend the money
- There are consequences for how we spend His money
- A budget will assist us in managing the money
- A budget will be the accountability tool to determine how we are managing the money

The First Steps of Budgeting

You read earlier that one of the main reasons to budget is that it becomes your record of accountability as a steward of God's money. A budget is simply a plan for how you spend your/God's money. For the remaining topics, I will refer to "your money". The assumption here is that you have already repented and re-committed "your" possessions to God and fully understand that it all belongs to Him. A budget is required to keep spending on track and to meet life goals. Worksheets for each step can be found in the Worksheet section at the end of the book. There are many excellent books written about finances that can provide in-depth detail and knowledge about the technical aspects of building a budget. The purpose of this is to guide you through the steps of the heart to building an effective budget and achieving your financial goals. We will be dealing with the heart of the matter. It will take time and effort to complete the worksheets and the budget, but it will be time well spent. Keep Proverbs 20:4 in mind when you want to quit at any point. It says that *"the sluggard will not plow by reason of the cold; therefore shall he begin harvest, and have nothing"*. In other words, if you are too lazy to plow, do not expect a harvest. If you are too lazy to put in the time and effort, don't expect any positive results. You must be willing to spend the time to pray, write down the answers to the questions asked, pull out all of your bills and go to work building the budget. If not, then do not expect to experience any changes by simply reading this book.

Step #1—Write Down Financial Goals and Priorities

Before you begin to prepare your budget, you will need a vision. An important step in this vision is to write it down. First, pray about the spiritual goals that God has for you and the financial requirements, if any, of each of them. You should include them as a priority in your planning. Use the Financial Goals and Priorities worksheet to record your financial goals and priorities. If you are married, this should definitely be done with your spouse. Think first about your short-term goals (next 12 years) and then your long-term goals. Below are some examples to help you get started.

Short Term	Long Term
Pay off Mastercard	Purchase new living room furniture
Daycare for baby	College fund for baby
Tune up for car	Begin part time work in 3 years
Vacation	Buy larger home
Begin full-time ministry	Assist Outreach ministry monthly

One goal that you should consider adding is to increase your giving to the church and those in need. Now that you understand how the giving principle works, this should be on your list. Another one of your short term and long term goals should be to eliminate all debt. In writing each of the goals, establish dates by which you will achieve the goal. The worksheet also provides a space for you to write your specific prayer regarding that goal to keep before you. Make sure the goal is very specific. After you have completed this, you now have a vision of what you are working toward. Without a vision, you will perish financially. Is God's vision for you included on your worksheet? If not, then you should strongly consider revisiting this planning session. I encourage you to keep a copy of this vision with you at all times. Keeping it before you will serve as a constant reminder amid all of the opposing messages you will be confronted with.

Step #2—Determine Current Spending Habits

The next step is to assess where you are right now. You cannot possibly get to your final destination until you know your starting point. You read earlier that it is wise to understand where your money is going in Proverbs 27:13. In order to assess your "as is" situation, you will need to record your current expenses. This is a very significant step in determining where your money is going. The easiest way to do this is to keep a daily journal of the money that you spend. Each day, record every dollar that you spend in a tablet or your day planner. It should be recorded on something that you will keep with you daily and can keep a running record of. It is very important that you record everything. Based on what you have learned in this book, you may feel conviction about certain purchases and that is good—but record them all. For each item, you will need to write down how much it cost and the name of the item. Keep this record for one month. It is very important that you record everything at this point.

At the end of the month review everything that you purchased and bills paid and begin to categorize them. See the worksheet on Potential Categories of Expenditures for examples of categories that may emerge in your list. These will become categories for building your budget. Keep in mind that a budget is a guideline. There may be one-time expenses that occur during the month, but you still want to capture those. For example, you may buy 3 birthday presents totaling $100 this month, but you don't anticipate any next month.

For purposes of your budget, you still want to plan for this type of expenditure. We will review these occasional expenses later. Once you have categorized your expenses for the month, add them to the appropriate category on the worksheet. Complete the dollar amount for all other relevant categories on the worksheet. What you have now is a view of your estimated monthly expenditures.

The Current State of Spending

Now that you understand and know where your money is going, you're ready to analyze each expense. The objective of this analysis is to determine why the expense exists, can it be adjusted and is it a wise use of the Master's money. This is a critical step to understanding and knowing the "state of your flocks". I strongly recommend that this analysis be done with sincere prayer and an open mind. The initial reaction to each expenditure is that it is justified and warranted simply because it may be a habit. Just because it is a routine expense for you, it is not exempt from this analysis. Now take a look at the completed worksheet. Does it tell you any stories at first glance? Do you see any unnecessary spending? You should feel a sense of accomplishment that now you know where your money is going!!! With the exception of your routine monthly living expenses, ask yourself the following questions about each expenditure—

Why did I buy that?
Did I really need that?
Could I have waited for that?
Did I charge it?
Could I have waited to purchase it?
Was it a necessity or want?
Did you pray about the expenditure? Should you have?
Was there an alternative to purchasing that item?

These are just some questions to prompt you to think about what value you associate with certain things and to identify the true root/spirit of your spending habits.

Typically, when a budget is built, we move right on to the next step of adjusting the current spending amounts. The spending analysis is one of the most critical steps in building a budget. If you don't realize and understand your spending habits, especially the detrimental ones, then you will build them right into your budget and continue on with the cycle. Remember that the tricks of the enemy are subtle. He does not want you to uncover the root of your problem because he knows that then the stronghold will lose its power. Go back to your list and answer the questions outlined above again, honestly. Ask God to reveal any hidden motives. Ask God for the grace to correct the spending pattern that needs to be addressed. This exercise should take a significant amount of time. If you finished this in 10 minutes, you have not devoted enough time to the review process. It could take as long as 3 days to complete this. You may review all of the expenses on the first day and pray about it. The next day you should review it again. God will answer your prayer and begin to reveal other areas to you. Invest the time in prayer and review to make sure that you develop the best possible budget. This process may also be painful, but hang in there, the reward is great.

Annual or Occasional Expenses

Expenses that occur annually or infrequently must be accounted for in your monthly budget. Although they are not paid each month, the expenditure must be considered. Omitting these can destroy a budget and begin a downward spiral in your finances. For example, Janice's homeowner's association fee of $300 is due January 31st. It is due the same time each year. Janice did not budget for this extra $300 that must be paid. By February 15th Janice receives the final reminder that the fee must be paid. Janice overextended herself on Christmas spending and feels the pressure to pay off her debt she accumulated over the holidays. Now this bill is due. Janice's option is to take the money from her savings account, charge it or take it from another bill that must be paid. All of her options could result in negative consequences and begin the decline of her financial state and potentially her state of mind. This is one area that cannot be omitted from the budget. If Janice had planned ahead for this expenditure, she could have saved a little each month toward the fee and the money would have been there when it was due. Other types of annual or occasional expenses that should be considered are:

Property taxes, tune up for vehicle, vehicle maintenance, vacation, birthday/anniversary gifts, school or sports registration fees, purchase eyeglasses.

Determine the actual expenditure or an estimate, divide by 12 and include this figure in your monthly budget. Since these expenses do not occur monthly, we typically do not consider how we will pay for them when they come up. Oftentimes, they are not considered when designing a budget. By factoring in the cost monthly, money is allocated to these types of expenses. Including the amount in your budget is only a portion of the requirement.

Simply writing the amount on paper does not ensure that you will not spend the money. In your checking account or checkbook, it will appear that this is "extra" money that you have each month instead of a reserve that is being built. For example, if your budget is $1,000 a month for all expenses and your income is $1,500, it will appear that you have $500 left. When you look at your budget on paper, you will see that $100 is allocated to vacation, eyeglasses and car repairs. You may keep this in mind for a period of time, but when a desire or need arises, it is easy to use a portion of the $500 for the item. It is easy because you actually see that the money is in your account and to equate this with the money being available. If you do this, then when the money is needed for the vacation, eyeglasses or car repairs, there is a deficit. It may become cumbersome to keep track of the reserve and distinguish it from actual surplus. If you have not developed the self-control and discipline at this point, I strongly recommend that you create a separate checking or savings account for the annual or occasional expenses. If you feel you have the discipline at this point, I also recommend a separate account for these types of expenses for ease of tracking and to avoid the temptation to spend the money. Once you open the separate account, which I will refer to as a Future Account, the money allocated in your budget for these expenses should be transferred monthly. So, if you estimate that your monthly allotment for the expenses is $300, then you should either write a check to the Future Account or have it automatically deposited to this account. Doing this will also give you peace of mind when anticipated events are approaching. You will know that the funds will be there to take care of the expenditure. Recall the number of times you have said "I don't know where I'm going to get the money from for ____!". Setting up this special account will remove that burden. As with every portion of the budgeting process, this step must be done diligently and consistently.

The Verdict

Now we are ready to see what your current financial picture looks like. Add up your monthly expenses. Add all of your expenses to obtain your total expenditures. Next, you can determine your Net Spendable Income by subtracting your expenses from your total income. A surplus exists when your income exceeds your expenses. If your expenses are greater than your income, then you are operating at a deficit. If a surplus exists, then I encourage you to pray about the direction that God would have you to send the extra money. It may be to save, give, invest or accelerate debt reduction. When most people see a deficit in their budget on paper, they do not readily believe it. This is because they see that their bills are being paid each month and they don't feel as if they are lacking in anything. This is another trick of the enemy—to keep us blinded to the true state of our finances. You may in fact pay your bills every month, but you may also be in debt and lack a real savings plan. Paying your bills on time each month is not an indication that you are not in a deficit situation.

I remember being comfortable making ends meet monthly because I was still able to eat out when I wanted to, buy clothes and pay my bills. What I didn't realize was that I was constantly withdrawing money from my savings account in order to do some of those things. In effect, it was not a savings account, but rather a holding account. This was an account merely to hold the money until I needed it. I lacked the discipline to do without the things if getting them required me to touch my savings account. My solution was to open up a mutual fund account that required a minimum withdrawal of $500. It required at least a second thought to access this savings account. We are lulled into a false sense that everything is okay because we are able to buy things. Upon closer inspection you will see that savings are being tapped into monthly or less than the budgeted amount is being paid on certain bills in order to meet other monthly obligations. We call this "robbing Peter to pay Paul". Because this is so easy to do, we become complacent month after month and the hole gets deeper and deeper.

Defeating the Deficit

There are only two alternatives to overcome the deficit—increase income or reduce expenses. Here are some things to consider if increasing income is the option you prefer.

- Will the method to increase my income interfere with my ministry, with my family or church?
- Will this require more time away from home?
- What will I have to sacrifice?

Beware of thinking that more money is the best choice. There are consequences that should be considered before doing this. If the strongholds of spending have not been sufficiently removed or overcome, additional income will only mask the problem and the issues will mount. The results can be devastating. I recommend pursuing additional income after prayer.

The most practical option for most people is to reduce monthly spending. In order to do this, you must evaluate each expense and determine if it can be reduced and if so, by how much. There are recommended standards by which many financial planners gauge acceptable spending. Howard Dayton, author of *Your Money Counts*, recommends the following percentage guidelines for each category. If you exceed the upper range in a category, that category should be analyzed carefully.

Category	Percentage of Income (after giving and taxes)
Housing	25-38%
Food	10-15%
Transportation	10-15%
Insurance	3-7%
Debt	0-10%
Entertainment/Recreation	4-7%
Clothing	4-6%
Savings	5-10%
Medical/Dental	4-8%
Miscellaneous	4-8%
School/ Child Care	5-10%
Investments	0-15%

The first thing you must do is to agree that all expenses are fair game and that nothing is off limits. Each expense must be scrutinized thoroughly in this process. This should not be painful if you honestly completed the worksheet to evaluate your current spending. Answering the questions in that section will assist in determining which items can be eliminated from your budget or reduced. Use the Spending Analysis worksheet to assist you in this critical evaluation process.

After careful consideration, research and prayer, you are now ready to begin building your budget. On the blank Expense Budget worksheet, write down the amounts that you will commit to spend monthly for each category. Once completed, determine your Net Spendable income again by subtracting your total revised expenses from total income. If your expenditures still exceed your income, then you must return to the evaluation phase to analyze your spending again. If you get to the point where you have a surplus, pray about it and either save, give or invest. Continue to adjust various items until your expenses equal your income.

The final and most critical step is to make sure that your budget is consistent with your financial goals. For example, if one of your personal goals is to buy a house in the next 3 years, your budget should support this goal. Your budget should reflect a plan to accelerate debt retirement and savings should be included. Take some time now to review your financial goals and verify that your budget supports the achievement of the goals. You have now designed a realistic budget to live by.

Maintaining Your Budget

First, let me say that your budget is only as good as the honesty you applied to each line item. If you were not honest with yourself about where you are, then your budget is built on lies. It will never work. It will cause frustration and you will not adhere to it. This exercise would have been a total waste of your time. In maintaining your budget, honesty is still the key. You need to be honest with yourself when you don't stick with it. You need to figure out why. You need to be honest when you have extra funds that are not reflected in your budget. You have to be honest with yourself; otherwise you will never improve your financial condition.

Developing a budget is only half of the goal. You must be prepared for the mental and spiritual battle to be consistent. I know that you feel good about having a plan to achieve your goals. You should feel a huge sense of accomplishment. You must also be aware that the enemy is not happy that you have a plan and that you are now well armed with the truth of God's Word concerning your finances. He is already planning how he can unravel what you have learned or place doubt in your mind about the goals you have set. **Remember to stay focused and rehearse the Word of God daily to build up your faith in these areas.** I recommend that you make copies of your budget and your financial goals. Put a copy in your kitchen, your wallet or purse and at work. Keep them near so that you can refer to them often. They will also serve as a reminder of the commitment you have made when the temptation arises to deviate from the budget. Keep in mind that a budget is not intended to restrict your lifestyle. It is a flexible, working document. It can be amended at any time. Anticipate a situation to come up within a week of developing your budget that will cause you to consider deviating from it. **Deviation from your budget is fine as long as it does not result in a significant detour from your financial goals or increase your debt.** Giving will be the first area that you will be tempted to reduce. You must resist this temptation at all costs. It will be easy to adjust the amount that you give because your mind may not be totally changed yet when it comes to giving. That's why I strongly recommend that you meditate on the scriptures in this book day and night. It will be a fight between your flesh and your spirit when it comes to this and many other areas of your budget. Remain vigilant, resist the devil and pray without ceasing.

Here are some tips to ensure that you maintain the budget you have created.

◆ First, you should pray about your budget and thank God for the wisdom that He has provided to you. You should pray specifically about the difficult areas of your budget. These are the areas where you believe that it will be a stretch to adhere to the amount allocated each month. You should ask God to give you insight and revelation on how to improve in that area. This is very important, because you built the budget based on the facts—income and expenses. But there was a huge element of faith built in when you reduced certain categories and added more to giving and saving. It looks good on paper, but you are naturally very concerned about whether you can actually make it happen. Prayer is the key.

◆ Next, for the first couple of months after the budget has been developed write down the actual amount that you spend in each category. Place these amounts in the appropriate budget category. This will help you to track how well you are actually doing against your budget. Again, I must reiterate that honesty is required to make this work.

◆ I encourage you to get an accountability partner. This is someone that you trust to be honest with you and to support you in this effort. This person should be a Christian and care about seeing you succeed in this endeavor. Share your budget and financial goals with them. They should also be your prayer partner specifically in the area of your finances. They may or may not be your prayer partner in other areas, that is your decision. I encourage you to have someone pray with you specifically about your finances because that area needs targeted prayers. You should share your budget struggles and successes. You should be able to share your intimate thoughts about your finances with this person. After you select your accountability partner, let them know what your expectations are. Generally, you expect them to discuss your finances with you, pray about your finances and challenge and confront you when you begin to deviate from the plan. This will not be an easy task. Most people don't want to get involved in someone else's financial situations. And most people don't like others telling them what they think of their financial situation. Both you and your accountability partner may have to change your mind about certain things before you begin this relationship. It can be powerful if the two of you consent to remain committed to the process and trust God.

CHAPTER 10
SAVING

A critical element of any financial picture is saving. There are very few people that place any emphasis on savings. Perhaps this is because there is so much consumer debt, that the debt is consuming the energy and focus of all of our finances. Without a sound savings plan, the debt cycle will continue and the abundant life is afar off. Many people have a savings account, but not a savings plan. What some of us have is really a holding account. We feel good sending money to a separate account called savings, but we continuously draw from the account instead of allowing it to build up. In reality, it is not a savings account. We are just holding the money there monthly and taking some of it out monthly—a holding account. Proverbs 21:20 says that it is wise to save—*There is treasure to be desired and oil in the dwelling of the wise; but a foolish man spendeth it up.*

Even the ant is recognized in the bible for its ability to plan ahead for the future as an example for us to follow. It is found in Proverbs 6:6-10

> *Go to the ant, thou sluggard; consider her ways, and be wise: Which having no guide, overseer, or ruler, Provideth her meat in the summer, and gathereth her food in the harvest. How long wilt thou sleep, O sluggard? when wilt thou arise out of thy sleep?*

The ant realizes that it will be more difficult to get food in the winter, so it gathers food in the summer. The bible says that the ant does not have a guide or leader that does this for it or instructs it to do this. It is simply a wise thing to have foresight and identify predictable things. Some things shouldn't need a leader or person to force us to do. Based on experience, the ant remembers what it is like to be hungry in the winter. It probably only takes one winter season to realize that it has to do something differently in order to avoid the same situation next season. The next step is to take action in the summer to plan for the winter.

Many of us have had the winter season in our lives where we have been caught without or struggling because we did not have the financial means to meet a need. Think about your last winter season financially. Was it painful? Did you have to go deeper in debt? Did you have to go without things that you needed? Did you have to settle for less? Recalling this experience should result in some action being taken to ensure that it does not happen again. No one should have to provide you with a thesis on why it is important to save. Like the ant, you need only plan for the next winter season—save. Many times we exit the winter season with simply a "Whew, I made it". That is not good enough and is shortsighted. Consider the ant!

A beautifully crafted savings plan is illustrated in Genesis 41:25-57. Here is the essence of the savings plan.

> **verse 30.** Joseph was aware, through the inspiration of God that a famine would come upon the land. *And there shall arise after them seven years of famine; and all the plenty shall be forgotten in the land of Egypt; and the famine shall consume the land; ³¹And the plenty shall not be known in the land by reason of that famine following; for it shall be very grievous.*

> **verses 47-49.** With the knowledge/revelation that he had, Joseph immediately planned for the famine when he had plenty. *And in the seven plenteous years the earth brought forth by handfuls. ⁴⁸And he gathered up all the food of the seven years, which were in the land of Egypt, and laid up the food in the cities: the food of the field, which was round about every city, laid he up in the same. ⁴⁹And Joseph gathered corn as the sand of*

the sea, very much, until he left numbering; for it was without number.

verses 56-57 When the famine came, Joseph was prepared. He had plenty to spare. *And the famine was over all the face of the earth: And Joseph opened all the storehouses, and sold unto the Egyptians; and the famine waxed sore in the land of Egypt. ⁵⁷And all countries came into Egypt to Joseph for to buy corn; because that the famine was so sore in all lands.*

The savings principle demonstrated by Joseph is a model for us to follow. During the times of plenty, we should not spend all that we have. We are supposed to save for the future. Some things we are aware of that we need to save for, but there are unpredictable things that can happen as well. We have to save for those things. Saving requires sacrifice. When you decide to save, you are also deciding to forego a purchase today so that you will have something to spend in the future. This is contradictory to the message that society delivers to us today. Society says that we can have it all and we can have it now. We feel that there are options out there to help us out of a financial crisis if we need it. It is sad that we expect to depend on loans or credit cards to bail us out instead of planning on using the resources that we currently have. Some Christians erroneously refer to Matthew 6:31-34 as a scriptural reason not to save. This is incorrect. The scripture reads

Therefore take no thought, saying, What shall we eat? or, What shall we drink? or, Wherewithal shall we be clothed? ³²(For after all these things do the Gentiles seek:) for your heavenly Father knoweth that ye have need of all these things. ³³But seek ye first the kingdom of God, and his righteousness; and all these things shall be added unto you. ³⁴Take therefore no thought for the morrow: for the morrow shall take thought for the things of itself. Sufficient unto the day is the evil thereof.

"Take no thought" does not mean do not think about it or plan for it. It is from the Greek word merimnao, which means do not be anxious. Remember that the context in which Jesus is speaking in chapters 6 and 7 is on how we express true spiritual worship. He is saying that when you are so consumed with the thoughts of material things, then you are not able to devote your mind to the things of God and thus worship Him properly. He is instructing us not to be consumed with the material things. We shouldn't allow those thoughts to dominate out mind and actions. I believe that savings will aid in meeting this command. When you are saving properly, you do not have the anxiety that comes along with meeting unanticipated needs. The same meaning applies in verse 34. We are not to be anxious about what tomorrow holds for us because it will have its own share of issues. Again, He does not say do not plan for tomorrow or meeting material needs, He is saying do not worry about them to the point that they become your priority. The priority is spelled out in verse 33. He says that the priority is to seek first the things of God.

The Emergency Fund

An emergency fund is a short-term savings strategy that everyone must employ. Everyone should have an emergency fund. There are many thoughts on how much should be accumulated in an emergency fund. The majority recommends that 6 months worth of living expenses should be saved in an emergency fund. This is also called a contingency fund. According to May Hunt, author of *Debt-Proof Living*, a contingency fund is

> A tangible hedge of protection. It is a pool of money that you can get your hands on in a short period of time, and is stored in a safe place that pays at least enough interest to stay ahead of inflation. ...It is a pool of money set aside for major catastrophes, when your only other recourse is to run for credit. It will be there if you lose your job or if your safety or health is at risk.(p.76)

Think about your last financial crisis. Think about the last time you *had* to use a credit card for a purchase and you were not able to pay it in full the next month. A contingency fund may have come in handy at that time. If most Americans were to lose our job or be suspended without pay for any reason for 3-6 weeks, we would find ourselves in dire straits. The reason that most of us don't think about this is because it hasn't happened—yet. Another reason is because we view credit cards as having cash or money available to us. This is a very dangerous mentality to have!! Let's think about the current financial state of the average American.

- Living beyond their means.
- Feel as if they have a certain lifestyle that they must maintain
- No self discipline toward purchases
- Lacks understanding of biblical principles on finances
- Do not give regularly

With these factors, and many others, in play, going without 2-3 paychecks will likely result in

- Anxiety about meeting daily and future known needs
- Cease any giving
- Deeper in the debt cycle since credit is the only option
- Cease paying tithes
- Inability to truly worship God due to all of the above
- Distracted prayer life

Wow! Look at how a simple lack of planning could result in serious consequences that can impact your spiritual life. If you don't have 6 months of living expenses saved at this point, begin saving for it immediately. If you have a savings account or mutual funds today, but it does not equal 6 months of living expenses, begin referring to it as your contingency fund and begin building it up immediately. Your true savings begin after your contingency fund is established and maintained. A key aspect of the contingency fund is that it is maintained. You must be diligent about not using the fund for all expenditures but for emergencies only.

How To Save

Now that you can sleep at night and not have to worry about "what ifs" because the emergency fund is being established, you should begin a consistent savings plan. It is important that you develop the habit of saving. Saving should be a routine activity. If you do not have a savings started, that should be one of your primary financial goals. Please add it to your goal sheet now if necessary. Even if you have a small amount saved, you should consider a goal to increase your current savings amount or the frequency that you currently save. A nice boost to your savings would be to commit your income tax refund or bonus to savings. The best way to ensure savings is allocated regularly is to write a check to savings after your tithes and offering or to have a portion of your income automatically drafted from checking to savings. Long term savings can be built through most company retirement accounts. Savings that can be used in the short term should be in an account that is readily accessible and should be used for planned expenditures.

A key point to remember is that there is a difference between saving and hoarding. Hoarding is saving solely for the purpose of retaining wealth for yourself. When money or things are hoarded, the purpose is selfish. The underlying motive in hoarding is to create sufficiency on oneself. This eliminates reliance on God, but rather on the things or money that has been built up. Jesus had a very definite comment and warning about hoarding in Luke 12:15-21—

> *And he said unto them, Take heed, and beware of covetousness: for a man's life consisteth not in the abundance of the things which he possesseth. [16]And he spake a parable unto them, saying, The ground of a certain rich man brought forth plentifully: [17]And he thought within himself, saying, What shall I do, because I have no room where to bestow my fruits?*

> *18And he said, This will I do: I will pull down my barns, and build greater; and there will I bestow all my fruits and my goods. 19And I will say to my soul, Soul, thou hast much goods laid up for many years; take thine ease, eat, drink, and be merry. 20But God said unto him, Thou fool, this night thy soul shall be required of thee: then whose shall those things be, which thou hast provided? 21So is he that layeth up treasure for himself, and is not rich toward God.*

The rich fool obtained great wealth and then applied his own logic as to what he should do with all that he had. The bible says that he said these things within himself. Again, it is a matter of the heart. What he said and the conclusion that he came to were a reflection of what was in his heart. He clearly viewed his wealth as totally his and not God's. Notice that he referred to the harvest as *his* fruits. This let's us know the mindset of the blessings he had received. He began this internal dialogue because he needed room to put the harvest—*What shall I do, because I have no room where to bestow my fruits?*. His intent was to first find somewhere to store the plenty that he had. It is interesting that no reference to thanksgiving or giving at all is mentioned. His thought was only on where he could put all that he had received. His solution was to create more work for himself. He decided to tear down his current barns and build bigger barns to store all that he had. There was no pause for prayer. To pray would mean that he acknowledges the Giver of the fruits and yield to Him for guidance on how to handle the prosperity. The man also incorrectly assumes that by building the bigger barns, he will have crops to enjoy for years to come. He assumes that the larger barn will keep his possessions safe. This is an earthly treasure that he has stored. It is definitely susceptible to moth, bugs and thieves. This is the mistake of many people that save without a purpose. The final conclusion he makes is that he can now take it easy and have a good time since his possessions are stored away. God calls this man a fool. He says that an account of his soulish actions is required immediately. An account of his stewardship is demanded suddenly. So, it will be with us all. When death comes to the man, who will get all of the riches he has stored in his large barns? The parable shows us that we don't know when we will be required to leave this world and whatever we have stored up will be left behind to someone, but it will not go with us. In summary, God says that a man that sores up treasures for himself and is not rich toward the things of God is a fool. He shall be separated from his things at some point and required to give an account of his stewardship. Hoarding is dangerous. Another important principle in this scripture is the lack of giving. The bible says in Matthew 6:21 *For where your treasure is, there will your heart be also.* This man's heart was set on keeping it all for himself; therefore he built barns to keep it all for himself. If his heart was set on the things of God, he would have had a mind to give away some of his excess. **Giving balances your saving. We are not to save at the sacrifice of giving. We are to give and save.** When we focus only on saving, our affection will be lead only in that direction. It will lead to selfish motives. Giving ensures that we are balanced in our heart toward the things of God. The difference between saving and hoarding is the attitude.

GETTING OUT OF DEBT

Pre-requisites

Now that you have a clearer understanding of God's perspective on debt, let's see how we can reverse the curse. The first thing that you must do to begin eliminating the debt is to repent. After reading the previous pages you have obtained knowledge and revelation about God's perspective on debt. You have learned the consequences of getting into debt and the requirement to expediently pay off the debt. Now that you have the knowledge of what the Word says about your debt and the repayment of that debt, you are accountable for doing what it says. The first step therefore is to repent. To repent means to turn away from sin, disobedience or rebellion and turn back to God. It means that you have changed your mind about a thing and have taken on the mind of God concerning it. So when you repent about past financial decisions, you are remorseful about the disobedience and sorry to God. Let's be clear, the sorrow that you feel when you repent is not because of the mounting debt that you are in. It is not for the things that you are going to have to give up to get back on track. This repentance is directed wholeheartedly towards God. You are sorry that you were disobedient and you now see your financial situation the way that God sees it. It is obvious when you are sorry towards God, because the next step is automatically repentance. Paul said in 2nd Corinthians 7:10—*For godly sorrow worketh repentance to salvation not to be repented of: but the sorrow of the world worketh death.* Repenting is a significant first step to getting out of debt. Until you view your debt the way God views it, you are destined to repeat the cycle. You must change your mind or current thinking about your finances overall.

The next step is to pray for wisdom and guidance to put together a very detailed plan to eliminate the debt. It will take the wisdom of God to reduce and eliminate your debt. Divine wisdom is required because there is and will continue to be a constant flow of materialistic and seemingly easy approaches to eliminate the debt. You will need to be able to discern the wise thing to do about your specific situation. You can be assured that once you have done these two things you will begin to be bombarded by offers to consolidate or obtain more credit. Surely, the enemy will make it appear that everything is needed *now* and you need the money or the things *now*. Your responsibility at this point is to follow the imperative and guarantee of James 4:7 *Submit yourselves therefore to God. Resist the devil, and he will flee from you.* Submission is something that **you** do. You must decide to humbly place yourself and your finances under the mighty hand of God. You must decide to subject yourself to the will of God and the command of God regarding your debt situation. You subject your thinking and your view of things to God's perspective. You lean not to your own understanding. While you are submitting yourself to God, there is still an accuser present. James said submit to God (period.). Then he says resist. The implication is that while you are submitting, the accuser of the brethren is present continuing on with his incentives, accusations, and suggestions. The instruction from James is to resist the devil. We are instructed to stand against these things. Doing this guarantees that the devil will flee from you. In other words, the suggestions and desires will ultimately flee from you. This has to happen the more you ingest the Word of God in your spirit regarding your finances. The more truth you have about your situation, the more submissive you will become. This will push out or force out the darkness the enemy attempt to bring to the situation. Light always pushes away the darkness. The offers will continue to come in the mail, yet the temptation will have fled. You will be able to throw them away or shred them without even entertaining the thought.

Proverbs 22:3 *A prudent man foreseeth the evil, and hideth himself: but the simple pass on, and are punished.* While this scripture is self-explanatory, I believe the King James Bible Commentary offers an excellent interpretation:

The prudent man is the man who looks ahead and anticipates impending difficulties. He then diligently hides himself in whatever refuge God has provided. The simple comprehend not the dangers that await them, and their destruction is assured in consequence.

You have read the many traps that can lead to this financial bondage called debt. It would be wise to take note of them all and hide yourself or avoid them. Notice that the wise man hides himself in whatever refuge God has provided. It is one thing to come up with your own solution to your debt problem, but the safe place is in the solution that God has provided in His Word. The simple has the same warning signs and instructions as the wise, but does not comprehend it nor take the time to understand and moves ahead. Remember in Hosea 4:6, the people were destroyed because they *rejected* the knowledge. Crown Financial Ministries offers 8 simple steps to getting out of debt that I wholeheartedly support. They really work.

1. *Give to God first.* The firstfruits of all that He gives us—the tithe from our gross income—must be our first commitment. Without faithfully fulfilling this commitment, all other efforts will fail.
2. *Stop all forms of borrowing.* This includes credit card use, personal bank loans, family loans, student loans, and all consumer credit. The sooner you stop borrowing, the sooner you will be out of debt
3. *Develop a balanced budget.* A balanced budget is the primary tool in any family's plan for managing money. If you are in debt already, the budget will need to be fairly restrictive at least for a while.
4. *Work out a pay-back plan with your creditors.* Most creditors are more than willing to work with people who honestly want to repay them. Make sure that every creditor gets something, but stay within the guidelines of your budget.
5. *Learn to trust God.* God knows what you need before you ask, so begin to trust Him for the things you need

but can't afford. Do not charge to get them; wait for God's provision.

6. *Exercise self-discipline as a lifestyle.* Curb impulses to buy. If it is not budgeted, don't buy it.
7. *Seek wise counsel.* Many people need assistance in establishing and maintaining a budget and working with creditors.
8. *Rely on God's Word.* Make all financial decisions based on the principles of God's Word, not on the world's financial principles and conventional financial wisdom.

It is critical that you spend significant time to determine how you ended up with so much debt. "So much debt" is relative. There is no magic amount that determines how much is too much to have. As a rule of thumb, most counselors will advise that personal debt should not be more than 10% of your income. Even with this rule, I may be considered within the guidelines with $1,000 of debt, but personally, that may be too much for me. I recommend using this guideline as a maximum, but your efforts should be toward totally eliminating your debt. Before you begin any debt reduction plan you have to fully analyze how you got into the situation. Think about the items that you have charged or used a loan to obtain. Were these items necessary at the time? Could you or should you have waited to save the cash? If you are like most of us, you cannot even recall what items you charged because they were small items. If you are unable to identify what items make up this debt, then there is a serious problem with your spending. Now would be a good time to review the earlier chapters on debt.

Discipline and wisdom are required to get out of debt and to remain debt free. Remember that there is a strong power associated with the bondage of debt. According to Proverbs 22:7 "the borrower is servant to the lender". This means that being in debt puts you in a slavery mind set and mode. You become obligated to the creditor. He then has power over you. He controls your other spending patterns. If you have to pay $500 per month in total monthly payments to your creditors, then that is $500 that you don't have available to give, help others or save. Since that $500 is required, the creditor controls a portion of your finances. Everything else has to be arranged around those payments. The creditor can exercise greater power by demanding payment or referring your account to a collection agency when payments are not paid consistently on time each month. They have to power to deny you additional credit. They have to power to impact your credit rating. It will require wisdom from God to break the power of debt in your life. One of the most effective holds that debt has on our lives is the anxiety and overwhelming feelings that it creates. When you are in debt, then it impacts the level of happiness you experience because you are limited in what you can do in life. If your debt does not bother you, then there is a deeper issue to be addressed. That would be rejection of the true knowledge concerning God's perspective on debt. You have to see it the way God sees it. It will take discipline to eliminate debt as well.

A key to getting out of debt is to stop buying things on credit. Based on your current spending habits this may or may not be a very difficult step to take. When you have debt, you may be comfortable with charging things. You must change your mind about this. Instead of using credit cards, commit to using cash only. If you don't have the cash, then you need to forego the item. Again, this will be very hard if you attached self worth, self esteem, social status or any other type of self-gratification to the item. When you attach these things to the purchase you then lose sight of the fact that charging it puts you deeper in the hole. All you see or feel is the positive self image that the item creates. This is why I encouraged you earlier to pray about every purchase. Submitting the item to God takes the decision out of your hands and requests for Him to intercede to assist you. Eliminating or reducing your debt may require a drastic change in your lifestyle. It is definitely something to consider. Depending on the amount of debt you have and/or how serious you are about becoming debt free, you should seriously consider a change in your lifestyle. Some people have been known to sell a car and become a single car family for a period of time in order to expedite their debt freedom. Here are some things to consider that will cause a change in your lifestyle but will speed up that day when you can say that you are debt free.

- Reduce or eliminate eating out
- Sell certain assets
- Reduce certain recreational activities
- Shop at consignment stores
- Switch to certain generic or non-name brand items
- Have a garage sale
- Scale back on entertainment activities (e.g., rent a movie versus going to the theater)

Keep in mind that any proceeds or income that is released by the change in lifestyle must be directed to the debt reduction.

A Debt Reduction Plan

After you have made up your mind that you are going to get out of debt and stay out, you have to commit to the work that it will take to do it. The next step is to write out a debt reduction plan. As long as your debt is in your head, then you will never get closer to reducing it. You have to come face to face with the debt to overcome it. You do this by writing down every debt that you have and the balance owed for each one. For each debt, also list the corresponding interest rate and the monthly payment. List the debts in order from the smallest to the largest amount owed. I strongly recommend that you pay off the smaller debts first. There are many financial counselors that will advise you to pay off the balances with the highest interest rate first. But remember that we are trying to break the power of the debt. If you target the smallest debt first, then you will feel a sense of accomplishment when it is paid off. This will serve as motivation and faith to continue with the plan. Now that you have a look at the whole debt picture, you can build the debt reduction plan.

In reviewing your budget, determine if you can afford to pay more than the minimum payment per month. This will really expedite your plan. If not, then definitely plan to apply a portion of any additional funds, such as overtime pay and bonus checks to the debt reduction plan. If you have access to the Internet, you can use the

Rapid Debt Reduction Plan tool found at www.debtproofliving.com. There you will find powerful tools to assist you with your debt reduction plan. If you don't have access to the Internet, you can still manage your plan on paper or in Excel. Create a separate sheet for each creditor. After each payment is made to a creditor, record the date, payment amount and remaining balance. You will see the balance coming down each month.

In order for this plan to work, you must continue to pay the same amount every month even though you see the declining balance. This is very important. When most of us see the balance going down and the lower monthly payment requirement we begin paying the lesser amount. Remember the plan is about discipline. You should continue with the monthly amount each month. Another critical step is to take the payment from the debt once it is paid off and apply it to the next debt in line. For example, Joan has paid off her Mastercard. She was paying $100 per month. She will take the $100 and apply it to the monthly payment of the next bill on her debt reduction plan. The total monthly amount that you pay for all of your debt should not decrease until all are paid off. The temptation will exist to take that money and apply it to you. You will definitely feel the accomplishment of eliminating one debt. You will then likely feel like you deserve that "extra money". Well, it is not "extra money" as long as you are still in debt.

Continue to pray about your debt reduction plan. Keep it before the Lord. Share your mistakes, concerns and fears with Him so that the Holy Spirit can minister to you in the required areas. Finally, stick with the plan. You will be successful as long as you view the debt for what it truly is—bondage. Believe that God is on your side in eliminating your debt because it lines up with His Word. Rest assured that He will honor your diligence and commitment in this effort. Make sure that you share your testimony of how God showed you the plan for debt freedom, you followed it and He delivered. You will surely be a blessing to others.

When you become debt free, it will be necessary to revise your budget. The monthly debt payments must now be re-allocated to other line items in the budget. Remember the earlier principles on giving and saving as you amend your budget. As you make the changes, you should also revisit your short and long term financial goals. Due to life changes, new goals may be necessary or the priorities may change. In addition, the long term goals may now be in the short term view based on becoming debt free. Reviewing this is required to make sure that the budget changes support the new direction. This is a good time to also review or begin investment strategies. The temptation will continue to be there to spend the former monthly debt payments but you should be well equipped by now to fight it off and win.

Debt Consolidation—BEWARE! CAUTION!

There are many companies that will proactively provide you with a non-negotiable check in the mail. This check will have your name pre-printed and a dollar amount. The details of the check may be taking out a home equity loan or loan consolidation to consolidate your bills to one lower monthly payment. These are very good options depending on your specific situation. But, in most cases, it is **not** a **wise** thing to do. With a debt consolidation, you borrow a lump sum of money to pay off smaller, lower debt for a lower interest rate. The purpose is to reduce the number of payments per month and ultimately reduce the overall amount paid via the lower interest rate. One benefit is that you develop a more focused view of the debt. Instead of several creditors, now there is only one bill per month. It offers a sense of fewer burdens even though the principal amount due has not changed. A debt consolidation can also take place when you transfer balances from one debtor or credit card to one with a lower interest rate. The principle is the same—lowering the interest amount owed.

On the surface, this appears to be a great solution or first step for reducing debt. There are however, many consequences that you must be aware of before you decide to consolidate your debt. First, you must have a clear understanding of the nature of the consolidation. When you consolidate the debt, you have merely moved it around and perhaps made the act of paying the debt easier, simpler and more convenient (now you write one check instead of four).

This step alone does not put you any closer to reducing your debt. In reality, now that you have lumped the amounts owed together, the payback time is extended further on the consolidation loan. This results in more being owed in the long run. A real danger in consolidation is that you mask the root of the problem. If you don't take the time to understand how you got into your current state of debt, you are destined to repeat it. A consolidation makes this very easy to happen. Once you have moved the balance to the consolidated loan, then you "feel" like you have paid them off because you now see a zero balance on the account. You even begin to think that you have made some progress. If you have not dealt with the corrupt spending habits that were outlined in earlier chapters, then the tendency to repeat the pattern exists. For example, you will continue to spend impulsively and feed your self esteem through material possessions. Consolidation makes this easy because you now have the space on your credit cards to fulfill these desires. The first thing to do to avoid this temptation and kill it is to close the accounts immediately after you have transferred the balance. Now, you will tell yourself that you need to keep them "in case of an emergency", but trust me, that is not a wise thing to do. Also, avoid the useless maneuvers to put the credit cards in a place that you can get to them if you need them for an emergency. That may work for a while, but whether the cards are in you purse, wallet, glove compartment or safety deposit box, you will always know that it is there and that it has an available balance. The next requirement is to continue to pay the monthly amounts you were paying on the individual debts. A main attraction to the consolidation is the lower monthly payment. Please be sure to analyze every detail of the proposed consolidation. It is very likely not the savings that you think it is. What do you plan to do with the difference between the old and new monthly payment? What do you think is the wise thing to do? If there is no specific urgent planned need for the difference, you must continue to pay the old monthly amount, even though it is not required. If you don't, you are just further delaying your debt freedom date. In summary, debt consolidation should not be used as a band aid to delay paying the debt or to simply give you some "breathing room" in your budget. If the details of the consolidation are favorable and the end result nets in less interest paid, you should consider it. This should not be an option for you upon the initial completion of your budget. Great discipline, discernment and knowledge are required to choose this option. Don't get caught in this trap!!! Proverbs 14:12 tells us that *There is a way which seemeth right unto a man, but the end thereof are the ways of death.* On the surface, it may seem right from your natural perspective to consolidate your debt, but be careful that it does not end in disaster. Apply diligence and obtain good financial counsel before making this decision.

Tithe and Offering or Pay off Debt?

I asked myself this question many times in the past. I'm sure that many Christians in debt have struggled with this question. For me, offering was not even a part of the equation. I struggled with tithing or paying off debt. I even got to a point where I became legalistic about the situation. When the amount that I was giving didn't equate to 10%, I stopped writing tithe on the envelope and labeled all of my giving as offering. That made me feel better. But, I was still missing it!! I'll share my logic with you.

- Surely, God would not want me to get further in debt by tithing instead of expediting paying off my debt.
- Once I pay these off, then I can tithe properly.
- God knows that I am doing the best I can.
- God knows my heart (I didn't realize how true this was!)
- If I tithe, then I can only pay the minimum monthly payment and I will never get out of debt.

Meanwhile, I continued to incur new debt, so this blew my second bullet point. I became very complacent in the amount that I gave and it became very routine and methodical (blowing the third bullet). Even when I paid off one debt, I took that money and spent it instead of increasing the offering. Does of any of this sound familiar? Just way ouch! There are many Christian financial counselors and secular ones that will advise you to focus on paying off your debts first and then resume the tithe and offerings. I however, respectfully disagree with this. The answer to this question is simple. Proverbs 3:9-10 says to *Honour the LORD with thy substance, and with the firstfruits of all thine increase: [10]So shall thy barns be filled with plenty, and thy presses shall burst out with new wine.* Since God is the First and the Best, we are to honor Him with or first and best. It really is that simple. The tithe and offering is not specifically mentioned, but rather to honor with our substance and the firstfruits of our increase. It belongs to God, not to the creditors first. Again, no specific amount is indicated in this particular scripture. You have to realize that it is the heart that God is after. If you give the tithe and offering while you are in debt, you are making a bold acknowledgment that you trust God and He is first. Now, I am not saying that you should tithe and give offerings in lieu of paying the creditors. You still have an obligation to pay them and you have in fact made a vow to pay them. Psalms 37:21 says, *"The wicked borroweth, and payeth not again: but the righteous sheweth mercy, and giveth.* It is a wicked person that does not repay his debts. Let's recall the earlier discussions on tithing and giving:

- Remember that tithing is a principle.
- It was the law to tithe.
- The tithe is the minimum
- Giving is the principle emphasized in the New Testament
- It is possible to give tithes and offerings with the wrong motive, yielding no results (2nd Corinthians 9:6-7)

With this in mind, remember also that it is the heart that God is after. I believe that there are several factors that you must consider when answering this question.

Have I placed other things ahead of the tithe and offering? This is a very important question to answer. If the reason that you are not able to tithe and give offering is because you have to pay your creditors, then that alone may be okay. You must repay your debts to line up with the biblical principles of repaying what you borrowed. If however, you use this as a reason, but you have other areas of your budget or spending where you can cut back in order to give, then you must question your true motive. For example, Jackie determines that she cannot tithe and give offering because "she is in so much debt that she doesn't have any money left at the end of the month to tithe". Jackie still does manage to spend $150 per month eating out and $100 per month on clothes. I suggest that Jackie changes her way of thinking about giving. I would advise her to scale back on eating out and clothes each month and plan to give the difference to God. Like many of us, she has determined by way of her spending habits that eating out and buying clothes are untouchable in her budget. Jackie would be the first to tell you that she loves the Lord with all her heart, yet her actions do not line up with her statement. God says to give to Him is to honor Him (Proverbs 3:9) and to withhold from Him is to rob Him (Malachi 3:10). As Jackie is spending each month, she is not really thinking about whether she is honoring God or robbing Him. She sees it as simply meeting her needs and wants. This is where our thinking has to change and be challenged. We have to transfer the ownership of money we have and the things we have to God. We have to see ourselves as stewards and accountable. The problem is also that Jackie did not *plan* to give. When you plan to give, you make it a priority. You force other expenditures to become secondary to giving. You make giving the untouchable line item in your budget, not the leftover amount. When you don't plan to give, you don't give. Jackie, like so many of us, stopped at "I can't give because of the debts" and never moved on to consider what she can give. Moving beyond "I can't" requires a purpose in your heart to give. I believe that when your heart is fixed on giving to God, the amount becomes secondary when you are under a pile of debt.

Have you Stopped Incurring New Debt? If you continue to incur new debt, then obviously your intention is never to give to God. Incurring new debt means that you have made a vow to the creditor to pay. Did you also make a vow to God that as soon as you were out of debt, you would give the tithe and offerings? Did you forget or did you simply say it and not mean it in your heart? You are obligated to the vow you made to God first. You must keep that vow first and then the vow you made to the new creditors.

After considering these, you must heavily layer your responses with the giving principles. Not giving anything is never the best financial solution. If you have received the earlier teaching on giving into your spirit, then you realize that not giving is more than likely the source of your financial situation. In summary, I believe that if the choice is to give tithes and offerings or to pay your debts, I say do both. You must give something. You must demonstrate to God that He is first. **You must begin to break the cycle of debt by entering into the cycle of giving which leads to increase—guaranteed.** If you can't pay the full tithe, give something and increase your giving as the money becomes available. Make sure that in what you give, you are sowing cheerfully and it does not represent leftovers.

If finances are that tight, after paying your debts, you must determine to give and allow reductions in other areas of your finances. If you spend the money on yourselves before giving to God, you will bring about serious consequences. Let's look at Haggai 1:2-11 *Thus speaketh the LORD of hosts, saying, This people say, The time is not come, the time that the LORD'S house should be built. ³Then came the word of the LORD by Haggai the prophet, saying, ⁴Is it time for you, O ye, to dwell in your cieled houses, and this house lie waste? ⁵Now therefore thus saith the LORD of hosts; Consider your ways.* Notice in verse 2 that the people kept saying that it is not time yet to build the Lord's house. They kept putting it off, but in the meantime they were spending the money on themselves. We have to be careful with putting off the things of God, because it will lead to complacency and ultimately unfruitfulness in our lives. We often put off giving to certain special funds or offerings until "next time". There is a danger in that. The problem was not that the people had built such fine houses for themselves, but that they did it at the expense of not building the temple. They did it instead of providing for the necessary things required to build the temple. They put themselves first.

God tells the people to "consider your ways". This is very important. God instructs them to reflect on what they are doing, think about how their actions line up with His commands and adjust their behavior accordingly. Verse 5 in the Amplified Bible reads: *Now therefore thus says the Lord of hosts: Consider your ways and set your mind on what has come to you.* He's telling us the same thing today. We must consider our ways and harness our thoughts when it comes to giving and stewardship. Proverbs 4:56 says that we are to ponder the paths of our feet. With the fast paced life of today, we often do not take the time to slow down long enough to thoroughly think about our actions. We tend to get comfortable operating in the same fashion, but God instructs the people to stop and think about what they are doing.

Verse 6—*Ye have sown much, and bring in little; ye eat, but ye have not enough; ye drink, but ye are not filled with drink; ye clothe you, but there is none warm; and he that earneth wages earneth wages to put it into a bag with holes. 7Thus saith the LORD of hosts; Consider your ways.* We often find ourselves in verse 6. God gives them some of the specific things they should think about. He says that they have worked very hard, yet they have not yielded much for their labor. He says that they never find contentment with the food, drink and clothing that they had. Finally, He reminds them that they do not have anything to show for the money they have earned. It is as if they have received their wages and put it in a bag with holes. He tells them again to consider their ways. This time, according to the Amplified Bible, He says *Consider your previous and present conduct and how you have fared.* For us, this is like working very hard every day and receiving your paycheck and you ask yourself the very next day "where did the money go?" Or, perhaps you received your income tax refund or a bonus and in a couple of weeks, you wonder, "what did I do with all of that money and what do I have to show for it?" You never seem to have enough. Have you ever felt like you just woke up one morning and found yourself in a tremendous amount of debt? Then, you look around your home to see what you have to show for it and you can't find it. That's what was happening in this chapter.

Verse 9—*Ye looked for much, and, lo, it came to little; and when ye brought it home, I did blow upon it. Why? saith the LORD of* *hosts. Because of mine house that is waste, and ye run every man unto his own house.* God begins to offer more in depth details to help the people understand what He put in place as a consequence for their actions. Here He says that He blew even the very little harvest that they brought home away. Again, He tells them that the issue He has with them is that they neglected the house of God, but ran eagerly to build up their own houses.

Verses 10-11—*Therefore the heaven over you is stayed from dew, and the earth is stayed from her fruit. And I called for a drought upon the land, and upon the mountains, and upon the corn, and upon the new wine, and upon the oil, and upon that which the ground bringeth forth, and upon men, and upon cattle, and upon all the labour of the hands.* God shows them that He is still in control and they still depend on Him for their sustenance. The people are not left to think that it was just a bad year, God specifically tells them that He withheld the dew and caused the drought. Many people today believe that the reasons they can't get ahead or make ends meet is because of the economy or the current state of war we are in. That may be partially true, but not necessarily the whole story. The truth of the matter is that they may be facing consequences for their actions. They will never get ahead until they hearken unto the voice of the Lord. Jesus plainly stated the summary of this entire lesson in Matthew 6:33 But seek ye first the kingdom of God, and his righteousness; and all these things shall be added unto you. You must read the awesome ending to this story. The people immediately obeyed the voice of the Lord and began to work on rebuilding the house of the Lord (Haggai 1:12-14).

Verses 18-19—*Consider now from this day and upward, from the four and twentieth day of the ninth month, even from the day that the foundation of the LORD'S temple was laid, consider it. [19]Is the seed yet in the barn? yea, as yet the vine, and the fig tree, and the pomegranate, and the olive tree, hath not brought forth: from this day will I bless you.* Just as there was a negative result of them not adhering to God's command to rebuild His temple, there was a positive result when they began to obey God. The result was God's commitment that He would bless them, yet while there was still evidence of the drought. This is akin to Malachi 3:10 where God promises to *open you the windows of heaven, and pour you out a blessing, that there shall not be room enough to receive it.*

I realize that I have provided a very long answer to the seemingly simple question of giving tithes and offerings versus paying off debt. The purpose was to give you several things to consider before making your decision. Please note that it is your decision. God has not specifically spelled out the answer in His Word for you on this. In my opinion, I believe that if your motive is to expedite your debt so that you can honor God with your giving, then you can forego the tithe for a period of time. Remember, you can say this is your motive, but your actions will indicate whether you are being honest or not. If you decide to take this route, I strongly encourage you to continue with some form of giving. This will ensure that you are activating the giving principle in your life. The bottom line is that it is a matter of the heart. You must however make sure you are aware of the consequences that go along with the decision you make in this area.

Check your credit report. A very important aspect of assessing the "state of your flocks" is to check your credit report at least twice annually. It is especially important when you are managing your debt to ensure that the account status is properly recorded. Just like with your character, your reputation is very important in making determinations about you. Creditors make assumptions about you based on whether you pay your bills on time or not. The data that is maintained by the credit reporting agencies is sold to various creditors. Although the credit reporting agencies are very reputable, they do have humans working there that can make mistakes. The account status may be inaccurate or there may be information reporting under your name that does not belong in your file. I experienced this quite frequently a few years ago. My maiden name is Smith. With such a common last name, I frequently had many records reflecting on my reports that were not accurate. I had to be consistent and diligent to have the information corrected. If I did not do that, then my credit rating would not improve. If I needed to borrow for any reason, then I would have a challenge due to the unfavorable credit rating.

Throughout this book, you have read that incurring debt puts us in bondage. If we incur debt, we should strive to pay it off quickly. So, the purpose of reviewing your credit report is not so that you can obtain additional credit, but rather to make sure that the information is accurate. If you need to borrow in an emergency situation then the stress becomes less due to the favorable credit rating. Some people do not worry about their credit rating because they know that someone out there is willing to loan them money. This is not the right attitude to have. Sure, there are many companies that will loan to those with poor credit history, but the interest rate is astronomical. As we learned earlier, when you pay interest on loans or credit card debt, you are not being a good steward. That is like throwing money away. Another reason to ensure that your credit report is accurate is to position yourself for opportunities that God may send your way. You may need to have excellent credit to start the business venture that God has placed in you. Under the Fair Credit Reporting Act of 1971, you have the right to request your credit report and review it for accuracy. Make sure you review your credit report after you request that an account is closed.

CHAPTER 12
OTHER FINANCIAL CONSIDERATIONS

T his chapter will provide additional insights on various aspects of your finances. More detail can be found in the books referenced in the Bibliography. This information is simply to give you some scriptures to investigate and thoughts to consider when planning your financial future.

Train Your Children

One way to ensure that your children learn from your financial mistakes and successes is to begin the train them at an early age. Proverb 22:6 tells us *to Train up a child in the way he should go and when he is old, he shall not depart from it.* This is the parent's responsibility. In order to do this however, the parent must first live the biblical principles of money management.

Society will surely do its part to educate our children on how to manage money or how not to manage it, but we should take the time to show them the plan that God laid out for their financial success. Early experiences in managing money will prove to be very beneficial in laying the foundation for success later in life. God instructed the Isralites to spend quality time discussing the Word of God with their children.

> *Therefore shall ye lay up these my words in your heart and in your soul, and bind them for a sign upon your hand, that*

they may be as frontlets between your eyes. [19]And ye shall teach them your children, speaking of them when thou sittest in thine house, and when thou walkest by the way, when thou liest down, and when thou risest up. [20]And thou shalt write them upon the door posts of thine house, and upon thy gates: [21]That your days may be multiplied, and the days of your children, in the land which the LORD sware unto your fathers to give them, as the days of heaven upon the earth (Deuteronomy 11:18-21)

Today, most children do not learn about the nature of money and how to handle it until they leave home. At this point, they are confronted with so many options and teachings that they become confused. They typically yield to the teaching that gratifies the flesh and that is the teaching of the world. In our society, credit cards are offered to college students. It is not as simple as an offer. It is seen as a way to get what they want and meet their own self esteem needs. It can facilitate moving them into the social class or status they desire to be a part of on the college campus. It is a scary thing. If they buy into this, they are setting themselves up for a financial disaster and a long-term burden.

The burden that it would create on young people is truly disturbing, but even more disturbing to me is that there is no over-whelming effort extended by the church to provide the biblical perspective on managing money to them. I believe that this is due to the blinders that Christians have regarding finances. The benefits and expectations of giving should be instilled in them at an early age as well. When we don't teach them about giving, we rob them of the benefits of giving. We have an awesome opportunity and responsibility as parents to begin the cycle of giving in their lives that will yield tremendous spiritual results for them.

Investing

Proverbs 21:5 *The thoughts of the diligent tend only to plenteous-ness; but of every one that is hasty only to want.* This scripture refers to the person that is diligent in their savings with the end result being that they have plenty. The hasty people will find themselves in want. The hasty person does not think things through thoroughly and reacts before a thorough investigation has taken place. Investments require diligence and research. The Bible warns against risky investments in Ecclesiastes 5:13-16. We are also encouraged to diversify our funds in Ecclesiastes 11:1-2 *Cast thy bread upon the waters: for thou shalt find it after many days. ²Give a portion to seven, and also to eight; for thou knowest not what evil shall be upon the earth.* Due to the uncertainty of the future, the scripture encourages us to divide the portion of the bread that is cast upon the waters. In other words, we should diversify our investments. Investing should be balanced with giving and saving. Recall the parable of the talents. The Master expects us to wisely use the resources that He has provided. Gaining interest on money is extremely wise. Investing should become an option for you after you have gained control of spending, giving is consistent, you are debt free and your contingency fund is established. Keep in mind that investing is also an alternative method by which you can build your contingency fund.

Beware of investing for the sole purpose of becoming rich. First Timothy 6:9 provides a warning for those that want to become rich. It says *But they that will be rich fall into temptation and a snare, and into many foolish and hurtful lusts, which drown men in destruction and perdition.* The word will in this scripture is very significant. It is the Greek word boulomai is not just an emotional fancy but indicates a calculated and planned procedure to get rich. The issue is not the desire to become rich, but that this desire supersedes the desire to follow God. Becoming rich, in this case, consumes the entire man and therefore God has become non-existent in his life. I don't believe there is anything wrong with wanting to be rich if the reason is to be able to give more to God, eliminate dependence on a salary or to help others. When these are the motives, then God is the focal point, not obtaining more for yourself just to "be rich". Before investing it is critical to identify your investment goals. Write down what you are trying to achieve and seek wise counsel to determine the appropriate investment vehicle to get you there.

First Timothy 6:10 tells us that you when you seek to get rich, you love money more than you love God. Look at the power that this temptation to get rich has—"...some coveted after, they have erred from the faith, and pierced themselves through with many sorrows.". It is strong and enticing enough that it has caused some to err from the faith in order to get rich. The result is that they bring pain and sorrow to themselves. In Luke 4:5-7 we see that this is one of the 3 temptations that the devil tempted Jesus with. *And the devil, taking him up into an high mountain, shewed unto him all the kingdoms of the world in a moment of time. ⁶And the devil said unto him, All this power will I give thee, and the glory of them: for that is delivered unto me; and to whomsoever I will I give it. ⁷If thou therefore wilt worship me, all shall be thine..* With so many temptations that he could have offered, he knew that he had to bring something that was extremely tempting and hard for man to resist. He knew also that he was the Son of Man, therefore divine as well. Knowing this, the devil had to bring out the big guns. We should be aware that this is on the top three list of things the enemy will bring against the people of God to draw them away from the faith. This shows us that one of the most powerful temptations that can be offered up by the enemy of our souls is to "have it all". We should always keep our motives before the Lord to ensure that we do not fall into this snare. We often hear people say that someone has "changed since they received the money". It's not the money, it is the snare that the love of the money has drawn them into. Paul cautions Timothy to avoid the desire to get rich and to instead pursue righteousness, godliness, faith, love, patience, meekness. Paul then encourages Timothy to fight the good fight of faith. The word fight is from the Greek word agonizomai which is an athletic term meaning "to engage in a contest". Paul tells us that it will be a fight to remain consistent and dedicated to the faith in the face of such temptation. But if we strive after the things of God first (righteousness, godliness, faith, love, patience, meekness) we would win the fight.

Please understand that I do not believe that it is wrong to get rich. It is wrong to pursue getting rich instead of pursuing God. Again, it is a matter of the heart. Getting rich has pitfalls and snares that we must be aware of and avoid. We must also understand the great accountability that comes with getting rich. Luke 12:48 tells us that "unto whomsoever much is given, of him shall be much required: and to whom men have committed much, of him they will ask the more."

Inheritance

Proverbs 13:22 *A good man leaveth an inheritance to his children's children: and the wealth of the sinner is laid up for the just.* We see here that it is a wise thing for a good man to leave a material and spiritual inheritance to his children's children. In order for it to reach his grandchildren, it must first pass to the children. He leaves enough material inheritance that the children can aptly leave some for their own children. In order to accomplish this, the good man must also leave a spiritual inheritance to his children. Providing spiritual guidance, examples and teaching to the children is how this is achieved. If you leave a material inheritance without the necessary training and teaching to manage it, then you have actually left them a curse. For they will be ignorant as to managing the new found wealth and a can fall into the snares referenced in I Timothy 6.

I don't believe that an inheritance should be a windfall. It should not be used to set the recipients up for the rest of their life. It could in fact end up cause a struggle when it was intended to help. A warning is given in Proverbs 20:21- *An inheritance may be gotten hastily at the beginning; but the end thereof shall not be blessed.* Wealth that is suddenly obtained can also suddenly cause negative things to happen. The end result is that it is not blessed or not a good thing. This is akin to get rich quick schemes. Providing an inheritance should not be done at the expense of living the abundant life now, giving, investing or tithing. The priorities have to be set up front. Leaving an inheritance should be built into to the saving and investment goals.

When it comes to a spouse, it is critical that both know how to manage money. Typically, only one of you will handle or manage the household finances. That is fine in order to ensure consistency. But it is vitally important that both are aware of the bills, the status of the debt, the credit ratings and the long term financial goals. If an inheritance is left to a spouse that does not have this knowledge, then that spouse will have a difficult time with the finances, especially amid the grief. I recommend that the spouses rotate this responsibility periodically. Even if for 1-2 months out of the year, you take care of all of the bills jointly. You should sit down and review everything together.

Another related aspect that we tend to neglect is the creation of a will. Everyone should have a will. If there is no valid will in place, the assets of the deceased are distributed according to the laws of intestacy. The will outlines how you want your assets or estate to be distributed. It must be written out clearly to ensure that your wishes are met. An attorney can assist with preparing and filing a will.

CHAPTER 13

GUARANTEED SUCCESS

Joshua 1:8-9 This book of the law shall not depart out of thy mouth; but thou shalt meditate therein day and night, that thou mayest observe to do according to all that is written therein: for then thou shalt make thy way prosperous, and then thou shalt have good success. ⁹Have not I commanded thee? Be strong and of a good courage; be not afraid, neither be thou dismayed: for the LORD thy God is with thee whithersoever thou goest. (King James Version)

In this scripture, you will find comfort and assurance in the steps that you have taken as you have read this book. For me, this scripture is the conclusion to the whole matter contained in these pages. I pray that it will bless you as much as it has blessed me in giving the assurance the process works and God is faithful. At this point in the scriptures Moses, the exceptional leader for the people of Israel, had died. Joshua was instructed by God to lead the people to the Promised Land. God Himself offered encouragement and expressed confidence in Joshua in verses 5-7. He promised to be with him every step of the way. This was a tremendous responsibility placed on Joshua. He had very big shoes to fill after Moses. I believe that God was sensitive to the emotions, apprehension and fear that Joshua must have felt. He talked to Joshua Himself. There was no middleman to offer words of encouragement God did it Himself. What an awesome God we serve! God, no doubt, also knew what Joshua would have to face in order to be successful in his journey.

After encouraging him, God then gives him instructions on how to ensure that he is successful in this great mission. After reading this book, you too have a great mission ahead of you. The expectations of Almighty God have been revealed to you and now you must live up to them. The mission will not be easy. The task is great. The debt is huge. The lifestyle is important to you. The habits are hard to break. The spending is out of control. The comfort zone is safe. The enemy is raging. God is fully aware of the task at hand. God, in the Person of the Holy Spirit, will be there to encourage you along the way. He will do for you just what He did for Joshua. He knows that encouragement is necessary.

He told him 3 things that he must do to be successful. Each of these applies to your financial success as well.

1. **This Book of the Law shall not depart out of your mouth**

   The Word of God shall continually be in your mouth. This means that when you discuss your finances, pray about them and review them, it should line up with the Word of God. Any financial decision should be based on the Word of God.

2. **Meditate on the Word day and night.**

   We are instructed to read and re-read the Word continually. To meditate is to read the Word until it becomes life to you. Meditation results on the Word influencing our thoughts and actions. Day and night means that reading the Word of God must be a priority. Time must be allotted to do this so that it is in you and will not depart from your mouth. For your finances, you should meditate on the scriptures outlined in this book. You should write them down, memorize them and rehearse them until your faith is built up in them. It will serve as a great weapon when the enemy tries to throw you a curve ball. You will have the Word of God to stand on to combat the lies he will tell you.

3. **Observe and do what the Word says**

   This is vital to your success. We are instructed to meditate on the Word so that we know what actions to take in our daily life. Reading and meditating on the scriptures is not done for the sake of knowing scriptures and being able to quote them. That becomes religion. We are to study them and do what it says. We miss the mark when we study the scriptures but do not apply them to our daily walk. This is a requirement. Jesus said in Luke 8:*21* *"My mother and my brethren are these which hear the word of God, and do it"*. Jesus was prompting their thinking on a higher level. He was referring to spiritual relationships with Him. He was saying that those that hear the Word of God AND DO IT, they have a spiritual family-like connection with Him. It is not possible to have a true relationship with God, if you do not obey what He says. We are also admonished by James in chapter 1 verse 22 to *"be ye doers of the word, and not hearers only, deceiving your own selves"*. This is where the majority of us fall short of our financial goals. We somehow are satisfied with just knowing what God says in His Word about financial matters. We have this false belief that knowing it will magically transform into a change being made in our lives and bank account. This is far from the truth. Many Christians are complacent today in just hearing the Word of God preached and reading it occasionally. The enemy is fine with that as long as you don't begin to execute the Word.

The latter part of verse 8 says that after 1-3 are accomplished "then you shall make your way prosperous…and have good success." There are conditions that must be met to ensure that you are prosperous and successful in your endeavors. Notice that the word is "shall" not "may". **It is a guarantee that if you keep the Word in your mouth, meditate on it continually and do what it says, you will be successful.** All of these steps are necessary for you to complete in order to be financially successful as well. Also notice that it says that "*you* shall make". The key to the success rests with you. God is guaranteed to do His part. But you have to take the time to do your part. *You* have to do the things required of a faithful steward. *You* have to give to the kingdom of God. *You* have to eliminate debt. All of these are instructions provided by the Word of God.

These instructions are followed by more encouragement. This battle that you are about to undertake to financial freedom may get discouraging at times, but be encouraged by the Word of God. I caution you not to look for too much encouragement for others. Until they change their mind about finances and view it the way God views it, then they are likely to think that you are going overboard and all that you are doing is not necessary. Regardless of what others may think, this is a spiritual matter. In 1st Corinthians 2:14 Paul tells us that *"the natural man receiveth not the things of the Spirit of God; for they are foolishness unto him: neither can he know them, because they are spiritually discerned."* Paul says that people that are walking after the flesh and not the Spirit do not welcome or accept the spiritual things. In fact, Paul says that he does not even understand them. So you see, those that are not praying with you or that are not walking in the Spirit will find your God-given strategy and tactics strange or unnecessary in their opinion. Don't be concerned with that. Stay on track and keep your focus on the goal. God will be there to encourage you. There may be times when you will have to do like David did in 1st Samuel 30:6—he encouraged himself. You will make it because God is on your side. He is committed to your success when you commit your ways to Him. Isaiah 55:10-11 shows us the guarantee of keeping the Word in our mouth.

> *For as the rain cometh down, and the snow from heaven, and returneth not thither, but watereth the earth, and maketh it bring forth and bud, that it may give seed to the sower, and bread to the eater: [11]So shall my word be that goeth forth out of my mouth: it shall not return unto me void, but it shall accomplish that which I please, and it shall prosper in the thing whereto I sent it.*

It is vital that you keep the truth about your situation constantly before you. The worksheets at the end of the book are designed to assist in that effort. In addition to that, I encourage you to be vigilant about studying the scriptures on finances. As I mentioned in the introduction, there are many scripture references on money, finances, debt, saving, planning, inheritance, etc. You should search the scriptures if you face a financial dilemma to see what God's perspective is on the subject. Once you have determined His view, then line up with the Word. You are guaranteed to be successful if you do. This will be critical to your success because the constant bombardment of advertisements, marketing ploys and other worldly influences will attempt to bring back old habits and familiar patterns. You have to abide in the Word so that you are built up in the truth. Do not underestimate the intensity with which the enemy will pursue your finances now that you have been exposed to the truth. Hold on to the Word and continue to fight. Remember that we have a money back guarantee (Malachi 3:10). God is faithful to His Word. We have nothing to lose and everything to gain. Begin to speak the Word aloud on your finances. This will also help to drown out the loud babblings of the enemy. Make no mistake that this is a war when it comes to gaining control of your finances. Be very clear on that. Paul tells us in 2nd Corinthians 10:4 that *the weapons of our warfare are not physical [weapons of flesh and blood], but they are mighty before God for the overthrow and destruction of strongholds.* This means that we cannot think our way to debt freedom or plan our way to a prosperous financial future. No, it will require supernatural insight and strength to do this. The goal in this scripture is not merely to survive the battle and allow the enemy to go back to their corner. It ways that the goal is to overthrow and destroy the stronghold. I encourage you to have this warfare attitude as you are working through your financial issues.

In this book, you have uncovered many of the strategies and tactics of the devil to keep you in financial bondage. You are now well armed to get off the sidelines and take an active role in your financial future. Just know that he will definitely pull out all the stops to keep you bound. Don't let this knowledge go to waste. Exercise your faith and take the first step. Complete the worksheets.

Begin praying about your finances. When you pray, pray God's financial words and principles to Him. He will recognize what He has already said. He is obligated to perform it for you when you meet the conditions that He set forth. Recognize that you can have what He says you can. Expect Him to deliver what you need when you need it.

Next, you will find a few true statements from God's Word. This section is included as a quick reference for you to refer back to when you need a "right now" word for your situation. You can read them as a reminder until you have the time to read the full text on the topic again. This is the type of book that you should read several times. There is so much to know about God's finances that you cannot retain it all in one reading. Get the truth in your spirit and watch God move!!!

A SUMMARY OF THE TRUTH

- God Is the Owner of everything (*Psalm 24:1, Psalm 135:6*)
- He has given us the authority to be **stewards** over His possessions (*Psalm 8:6*)
- Money is morally neutral. It has no inherent value.
- If your love and devotion is to obtaining money in order to get rich, then your loyalties are divided. You cannot be devoted to God and money at the same time. (*Luke 16:13*)
- A **steward** is one is entrusted with caring for a superior's goods
- Not doing anything with what God has given to us is just as bad as mismanaging it. (*Proverbs 18:9, Matthew 25:14-30*)
- God does not own or desire only the tenth or tithe, but He owns 100%.
- Transfer the title to every item in your possession to God right now
- Jesus came to fulfill the law. There is a spiritual intent behind **tithing.** (*Matthew 23:23*)
- Tithing is one form of giving.
- It is an expectation that Christians give (*2nd Corinthians 9:6-7*)
- **Giving** is a matter of the heart
- We are expected to **give regularly** (*1st Corinthians 16:2*)
- Your attitude in giving is important and noticed by God

- There is a relationship between how much you give and what you receive

- By being **obedient and willing to give** to God first, your earthly needs will be met *(2nd Corinthians 9:8)*

- The **Giving Cycle**
  God supplies the needs and abundance to His people
  - Out of thanksgiving and obedience to God, His people give generously
  - Giving results in material needs being met
  - Giving results in abundant blessings
  - You are able to give more out of your abundance
  - You are able to assist in meeting the needs of others
  - Through your giving others give thanks to God
  - God is glorified!!!

- There are **motives or desires behind our spending** that must be discerned and addressed in order to build an effective budget.

- **Contentment** is a learned behavior *(Philippians 4:10-13)*
  We must learn to be content through the experiences that we have. We must learn to make the best of whatever state we find ourselves in. It requires Divine ability to learn contentment. It is through the Christ that we are strengthened in this area.

- You are in **debt** when you obtain money that you did not earn. This can be through a line of credit, credit cards or loan from friend of family member.

- When you owe a **debt**, you become a **servant** to the creditor. *(Proverbs 22:7)*

- You are considered wicked if you borrow and do not repay. *(Psalm 37:21)*

- When debt is incurred, there is an assumption that there will be income in the future to repay. *(James 4:13-15)*

- How we treat our finances overall is a **matter of the heart**. *(Matthew 6:19-24)*

- **Biblical prosperity**
  - requires obedience *(Deuteronomy 28:1-13)*
  - comes with warnings *(Deuteronomy 8:10-18, 1st Timothy 6:17-19))*
  - involves giving *(Proverbs 3:9-10)*
  - God is sovereign and can make the final decision on who prospers and who does not *(1st Chronicles 29:11-12)*

- A **budget** is a financial roadmap. It is the accountability tool for good stewards. *(Proverbs 27:23)*

- It is important to write down financial goals and priorities before beginning a budget.

- It is wise to have a **savings** plan *(Proverbs 6:6-10)*

- There is a difference between **saving and hoarding**. *(Luke 12:15-21)*

- Complete honesty is required when developing a budget.

- Beware of debt consolidation

- Getting out of debt (Proverbs 22:3)
  - Repent and Repay
  - Put together a debt reduction plan
  - Resist impulses to buy
  - Stop borrowing

- We are required to **train our children** to be financially aware and successful. *(Proverbs 22:6, Deuteronomy 11:18-21)*

WORKSHEETS

MY FINANCIAL THOUGHTS

Proverbs 23:7 *For as he thinketh in his heart, so is he: Eat and drink, saith he to thee; but his heart is not with thee.*

Write your answers to the questions below. In order to gain the benefit that these questions are designed to provide, you must be totally honest in your responses. The questions are to assist you in determining your current financial state of mind. When you face that, you can then begin to unravel it and replace or supplement it with Godly principles.

1. What do you think God's perspective is on being rich?

2. Do you believe that God is only concerned about whether you give the tithe or not?

3. Do you believe that it is not possible to have a lot of money and serve God? Why or why not?

4. Do you believe that tithing and offerings is all that God expects for us to give?

5. Do you view the money that you have as your money?

6. Do you believe that if you had a particular amount of money your life would be easier in terms of financial stress?

7. Based on your experiences and interpretation, what expectations does the church communicate regarding finances?

8. How do you feel about and treat the offering time at church? **9.** What does stewardship mean to you?

10. Why do you think you are in the current financial state that you are in?

GAINING AND MAINTAINING THE PROPER PERSPECTIVE

- *Psalm 24:1 The earth is the LORD's, and the fullness thereof.*
- *Psalm 8:6 Thou madest him to have dominion over the works of thy hands; thou hast put all things under his feet.*

Write your answers to the questions below. The questions are designed to assist you in summarizing what you have learned and to translate that into actions. Answer the questions in your own words.

1. What does stewardship mean?

2. What does God expect from us in terms of stewardship?

3. If God were to ask for an interim account of your stewardship, would He be pleased with your track record? Why or why not? Remember not to offer excuses like the wicked steward did in Matthew 25:14-30.

4. If the answer to question #3 is no, then list the items that you have not been a good steward over. For each item, list the things that you think you can do differently to improve in the care of those things.

5. Do you desire to be rich? Why or why not?

6. What are the potential dangers of the desire to be rich?

7. Looking at your life, what are the priorities that you have established for yourself? List them in order of importance. Don't answer this question with your head or your heart. This question has to be answered according to the behaviors your exhibit.

   For example, if you work so many hours per week that your family life and spiritual life are not equally balanced, then work is a priority for you. If you are working so much so that you can get the house you have always wanted, then getting the house becomes the priority. If you function daily just to make ends meet, then your priority is to just make it through life. If you spend planned time daily with the Lord, then that may be your priority. If you are consumed with your child(ren) extra curricular activities, then they are the priority.

8. Review the list you created above. It will tell you what is really important to you. How accurate is it? Are you satisfied with the priorities you are living out? What changes should you make? What daily changes will you make? How will you make them and when?

9. Share the results of #8 with your spouse if you are married. If single, share them with someone that you trust. They will become your accountability partner. It should be someone that loves you enough to disagree with you and to remind you when you are going astray. Pray with them about your renewed commitment.

10. Meditate daily on the following scriptures.

- Psalm 24:1 *The earth is the LORD's, and the fullness thereof.*
- Psalm 135:6 *Whatsoever the LORD pleased, that did He in heaven, and in earth, in the seas, and all deep places.*
- Psalm 8:6 *Thou madest him to have dominion over the works of thy hands; thou hast put all things under his feet.*
- I Timothy 6:8 *And having food and raiment, let us be therewith content.*
- 1 Corinthians 4:2 *Moreover it is required in stewards, that a man be found faithful.*

RENEWED THINKING—GIVING

1st Thessalonians 2:13 *For this reason we also thank God without ceasing, because when you received the word of God which you heard from us, you welcomed it not as the word of men, but as it is in truth, the word of God, which also effectively works in you who believe.*

Listed below is a summary on the teaching provided on giving. This principle is so important that I want to ensure that you receive all of it. Incorporated in the summary are affirmations that you should begin to read daily until your behavior (flesh) begins to implement what it says. The objectives are to change your mind to the mind of Christ regarding giving and to prompt you to begin giving more. By rehearsing this in your spirit, you begin to accept it as the truth. Reciting the truth daily will result in increased truth in your spirit and your flesh ultimately has to line up. This is necessary because you will continue to hear materialistic and selfish worldly methods daily. This will begin to drown out those messages!!

1. Read Exodus 35
   - Whosoever is of a willing heart was asked to give.
   - The people responded immediately. They believed it was God speaking, therefore no analysis of the instructions was necessary.
   - We are to respond in the same way when we know that God is instructing us to give.
   - They gave generously.

2. 2nd Corinthians 9:6-7—*But this I say, He which soweth sparingly shall reap also sparingly; and he which soweth bountifully shall reap also bountifully. 7Every man according as he purposeth in his heart, so let him give; not grudgingly, or of necessity: for God loveth a cheerful giver.*

- I recognize that there is a relationship between how much I sow and how much I reap.
- The amount that I give is personal.
- Giving is a matter of the heart.
- The attitude behind my giving is noticed by God.
- I will give cheerfully.

3. Proverbs 11:24—*There is he that generously scatter abroad, and yet increase more; there are those who withold more than is fitting or what is justly due, but it results only in want.*
   - The more I give, the more I will receive.
   - I will not continue in lack because I will give what is in my power to give. I will not withhold back anything in this area.

4. Luke 6:38—*Give, and it shall be given unto you; good measure, pressed down, and shaken together, and running over, shall men give into your bosom. For with the same measure that ye mete withal it shall be measured to you again.*

   Malachi 3:10 *Bring ye all the tithes into the storehouse, that there may be meat in mine house, and prove me now herewith, saith the LORD of hosts, if I will not open you the windows of heaven, and pour you out a blessing, that there shall not be room enough to receive it.*
   - I believe the Word of God on the topic of giving.
   - I believe that God will give me such an overflow of blessings when I am obedient in giving if my heart is right.

5. 1st Corinthians *16:2 Upon the first day of the week let every one of you lay by him in store, as God hath prospered him, that there be no gatherings when I come.*
   - I will give regularly.
   - I will plan to give.

6. 2nd Corinthians 9:10 *Now he that ministereth seed to the sower both minister bread for your food, and multiply your seed sown, and increase the fruits of your righteousness;*
   - I expect increase as a result of my giving.

7. 2nd Corinthians 9:11 *Thus you will be enriched in all things and in every way, so that you can be generous, and [your generosity as it is] administered by us will bring forth thanksgiving to God* (Amplified Bible).
   - When I receive my increase, I will continue to give.
   - It is an expectation that I continue to give from my increase.
   - God is glorified in my giving.

8. The cycle of giving
   - God supplies the needs and abundance to His people
   - Out of thanksgiving and obedience to God, His people should give generously.
   - Giving results in material needs being met
   - Giving results in abundant blessings
   - You are able to give more out of your abundance
   - You are able to assist in meeting the needs of others
   - Through your giving, others give thanks to God
   - God is glorified!!!

THE HEART OF THE MATTER—SPENDING ANALYSIS

Matthew 6:19-21 *Lay not up for yourselves treasures upon earth, where moth and rust doth corrupt, and where thieves break through and steal: But lay up for yourselves treasures in heaven, where neither moth nor rust doth corrupt, and where thieves do not break through nor steal: For where your treasure is, there will your heart be also.*

1. List the last 5 items you purchased over $50. (This can be items that you paid cash, charged, leased or rented)

2. Why did you need or want the item? You must be very honest here to get the desired results.

3. Are you currently using them regularly?

4. Was it a planned or budgeted item?

5. If the item was not purchased with cash, could you have waited to get the item until you had the cash to pay for it?

6. Were there less expensive options?

7. Do you regret making the purchase?

8. Did you pray about the purchase ahead of time? Should you have?

9. Can you think of any negative impacts to this purchase? (increased amount of debt, another bill to pay, new monthly payment not available to give now)

10. What are the benefits of having this item?

MY FINANCIAL GOALS AND PRIORITIES

My spiritual goals are

_____

_____

_____

_____

_____

_____

_____

Long Term and Short Term Financial Goals

- Long term (2 yrs. and beyond)
- Short term (less than 2 yrs.)
- Date—the date by which you would like to plan to achieve the goal
- Where appropriate, include dollar amounts

GOAL	DATE

My Specific Prayer *(Write out your specific prayer(s) for your goals.)*

_____

_____

_____

_____

_____

_____

_____

_____

_____

_____

_____

Keep a copy of this in your financial files at home, in your purse/wallet and in your daily planner/organizer. Refer to this worksheet regularly to ensure that your actions support the successful achievement of your goals.

POTENTIAL EXPENSE CATEGORIES

Housing $_____
Mortgage or Rent   _____
Insurance   _____
Property Taxes   _____
Electricity Gas   _____
Water   _____
Sanitation   _____
Telephon   _____
  Local/Long Distance   _____
  Wireless   _____
Lawncare   _____
Pest Control   _____
Cleaning and Supplies   _____
Other _____   _____
Other _____   _____

Food $_____

Transportation $_____
Auto payments   _____
Gas   _____
Insurance   _____
Maintenance/Repair   _____
License/Taxes   _____
Other   _____

Insurance $_____
Life   _____
Medical   _____
Other   _____

Debts $_____
Credit Cards   _____
Loans   _____

Entertainment/Recreation $_____
Eating Out   _____
Babysitters   _____
Vacation   _____
Video Rental   _____
Movies   _____
Birthday gift   _____

Clothing $_____
Adults   _____
Children   _____

Savings $_____

Medical Expenses $_____
Doctor   _____
Specialists   _____
Prescriptions   _____
Other   _____

School/Child Care $_____
Tuition   _____
Supplies   _____
Day Care   _____
Supplies   _____
Lunch   _____
Other _____   _____
Other _____   _____
Other _____   _____
Other _____   _____

Miscellaneous $_____
Toiletry, Cosmetics   _____
Barber, beauty   _____
Laundry   _____
Subscriptions   _____
Christmas Gifts   _____
Inernet   _____
Cable/Satellite   _____
Other   _____
Other   _____

Investments $_____

_____   _____
_____   _____
_____   _____
_____   _____
_____   _____

EXPENSES ANALYSIS

Expense	Questions to Ask/ Options to Consider
Housing	
Mortgage or Rent	Is refinancing to a lower rate an option? Move to obtain lower mortgage?
Insurance	Shop around for rates.
Telephone Local/Long Distance	Monitor long distance calling. Call local phone company to review monthly package options. Use wireless phone "free long distance" minutes for all long distance calls.
Wireless	Make sure that you are on the most effective plan. Use the phone less and lower plan.
Lawncare	Do you know anyone that does this? Can you do it? Ask friends and neighbors for references.
Pest Control	Shop around.
Cleaning and Supplies	Most dollar stores carry the same products for lower price.
Food	
Groceries	Are you throwing out food because it spoils? Use coupons? Don't overstock pantry.
Transportation	
Auto payments	Refinance

Gas	Is carpooling an option?
Insurance	Shop around.
Maintenance/Repair	Do not miss scheduled maintenance.

Debt

Credit Cards	Request lower interest rate
Loans	Request lower interest rate

Entertain/Recreation

Eating Out	Plan meals. Take your lunch. Eat before leaving home. Pack snacks for short trips.
Vacation	Plan in advance and shop around
Video Rental	Limit
Birthday gift	Purchase in advance when on sale
Birthday party	Are there cheaper options?

Clothing

Adults	Name brands? Necessity or want?
Children	Name brands? Shop sensibly considering their growth rate.

Savings

School/Child Care

Tuition	Consider all options. Research schools and county rules.
Supplies	Plan ahead.
Lunch	Plan ahead.

Miscellaneous

Toiletry, Cosmetics	Shop around. Use coupons.
Barber, beauty	Can frequency be adjusted?
Subscriptions	Can any be eliminated?

Christmas Gifts	Plan ahead. Buy throughout the year. Be creative.
Internet	Shop around.
Cable/Satellite	Shop around.
Investments	Seek wise counsel.

BIBLIOGRAPHY

Alcorn, Randy. *Money Possessions and Eternity*. Wheaton, IL: Tyndale House Publishers, Inc. 2003.

Dayton, Howard. *Your Money Counts*. Longwood, Florida: Crown Ministries, Inc. 1996

Hunt, Mary. *Debt-Proof Living: The Complete Guide to Living Financially Free*. Nashville, TN: Broadman & Holman Publishers, 1999.

Nichols, Dwight. *God's Plans for your Finances*. New Kensington, PA: Whitaker House, 1998.

Printed in the United States
47668LVS00003B/304-339